# *A Son for Glory*
## Job Through New Eyes

Toby J. Sumpter

Athanasius Press

Monroe, Louisiana

A Son for Glory: Job Through New Eyes
Copyright © 2012 by Athanasius Press
205 Roselawn
Monroe, Louisiana 71201
www.athanasiuspress.org

ISBN: 978-0-9842439-8-3 (softcover)

All rights reserved. No part of this publication may be reproduced, stored in a retrieval system, or transmitted in any form or by any means — electronic, mechanical, photocopy, recording, or any other — except for brief quotations in printed reviews, without the prior permission of the publisher.

This publication contains The Holy Bible, English Standard Version®, copyright © 2001 by Crossway Bibles, a publishing ministry of Good News Publishers. The ESV® text appearing in this publication is reproduced and published by cooperation between Good News Publishers and Athanasius Press and by permission of Good News Publishers. Unauthorized reproduction of this publication is prohibited.

The Holy Bible, English Standard Version (ESV) is adapted from the Revised Standard Version of the Bible, copyright Division of Christian Education of the National Council of the Churches of Christ in the U.S.A. All rights reserved.

English Standard Version®, ESV®, and the ESV® logo are trademarks of Good News Publishers located in Wheaton, Illinois. Used by permission.

# Contents

|     | Preface | v |
| --- | --- | --- |
| 1   | Introduction | 7 |

### Part One | The Prologue

| 2 | Adam and Sons<br>*Job 1:1–5* | 23 |
| --- | --- | --- |
| 3 | Fathers, Sons, and the Satan<br>*Job 1:6–12* | 33 |
| 4 | From Good to Very Good<br>*Job 1:13–22* | 51 |
| 5 | Faith That Receives and Cries Out<br>*Job 2–3* | 67 |

### Part Two | The Dialogues

| 6 | The Wind Blows<br>*Job 4–13* | 85 |
| --- | --- | --- |
| 7 | Justice in the Grave<br>*Job 14–21* | 111 |
| 8 | Crowned With Wisdom<br>*Job 22–31* | 131 |
| 9 | Childish Wisdom<br>*Job 32–37* | 155 |
| 10 | The Storm Speaks<br>*Job 38–42* | 171 |
| 11 | A Son in Glory<br>*Job 42* | 187 |

# Preface

The book of Job is a storm. It is a storm of words, a storm of worlds colliding. While the narrative opens peacefully enough, before the first chapter is out, the wind has begun to blow. Storms strike the house of Job with horrific precision and vehemence. Before the book is over, Job comes face to face with Yahweh in the whirlwind. Even as Job is comforted in the closing verses of the book, one notices that he is windblown and storm-struck, but he emerges with a kind of wisdom and courage that every Christian is called to emulate and seek. Job has grown up into greater glory, greater maturity. He is a son who bears the marks in his body of communion with the God of the universe, a family resemblance to the Father, Son, and Spirit.

Because of this, Job is not everyone's favorite book of the Bible. It is a long book in which little happens aside from long speeches. The "action" is largely found in the first two chapters and the last chapter. As many have pointed out, if you cut the middle dialogues and put the prologue and epilogue together, you actually have a fairly coherent (and short) fairy tale that seems to communicate the same morals, making the same theological point. Job doesn't go that way. Job is long-winded, filled with long speeches and argument which don't seem to get anywhere. Perhaps most frustrating is the fact that we are told at the end of the book that the three friends are "wrong." Thus, a good portion of the book of Job is wrong. Why would the Spirit inspire a book of the Bible which gives so much air time to bad advice?

Job is also an avoided book of the Bible because it is terrifying. The book of Job is about a faithful and righteous man who is struck down by God. Even though Job is restored at the end of the story, no one really wants to go through that. We pay lip service to holiness and wisdom, but the cost seems too great. Who is willing to be struck like that? And God seems far too eager for this. God points out his servant Job to Satan in a way that we hope and pray he will never do to us. We cultivate a studious avoidance of the book of

Job in much the same way that we avoid praying for things like "patience." For it is a well known fact that our God loves to give such things, and his usual method is to give us circumstances in which we will have to learn patience. In the same way, many are afraid of Job and of learning the lessons of Job because we fear that God will notice us. We fear that he will love us like he loved Job, and that he will strike us.

As the Church meditated on the book of Job down through the centuries, she has realized (if reluctantly at times) that we are not dealing with a different God or a different side of our God. Rather, this is the same God who came for us in Jesus, the same God who noticed his beloved Son in the waters of the Jordan, the same God who struck this beloved Son on the cross and then raised him to glory in the resurrection. This Jesus, this Son who was struck, does not offer an alternative route. He plainly insists that if anyone will follow him, he must deny himself and take up his cross. Yet he does not merely call his sons to the cross. His own death, resurrection, and ascension effectually draw us, accomplishing in us the very thing he calls us to by the mighty working of his Spirit.

The book of Job is not an optional portion of the Bible. It does not present a path of wisdom and patience that is for super-holy Christians. The book of Job is nothing less than the gospel of Jesus Christ. It is the good news that God comes for his people, but he does not come on our terms. He does not come and leave us untouched or unchanged. He comes to transfigure us—to cleanse us, transform us, and draw us up into his glorious presence. He comes in the storm of his presence, and he blows upon us and our families and our stories; he blows upon them until they glow with the fire of his glory. The act of reading and studying the book of Job is an invitation into that storm. It is a call to enter the whirlwind, to walk into the hurricane of his glory.

# 1

## INTRODUCTION

The book of Job is one of the most widely read books of the Bible. Considered from literary, philosophical, biblical, and linguistic angles, Job provides a number of fascinating avenues of research and consideration. Robert Alter says that Job is "arguably the greatest achievement of all biblical poetry."[1] Thus, from a literary standpoint, Job garners attention. From Melville's *Moby Dick* to Johann Wolfgang von Goethe's *Faust*, one finds scenes, characters, and parallels derived from the biblical text of Job. The story of Job is most famous for its presentation of suffering and evil, and specifically, the revelation that God is involved in suggesting and allowing the suffering of Job. This makes the book of Job significant for theological and philosophical questions of *theodicy*, which seek to

---

1. Robert Alter, *The Art of Biblical Poetry* (New York, NY: Basic Books, 1985), 76.

# Introduction

justify the goodness of God in the face of evil, and ask, is there justice in the world, and can God be criticized for his actions? With the same token, those of the Augustinian and Reformation traditions see the book of Job as proof of God's providence and goodness. The resolution of Job's hardships seems to point to the overarching good intentions and resolve of the Creator God.

Too frequently, however, the text of Job is sacrificed on the altars of sentimentalism, moralism, and various strains of modernism. For examples of the first two, Job is regularly cherry-picked for quotations to put on "Christian" motivational calendars and devotional booklets. On this reading, Job's initial responses to the tragedies that befall him are a pattern for Christian faith and bear witness to the sovereignty and providence of God. "Shall we indeed accept good from God, and shall we not accept adversity?" Then only verses later, Job unleashes one of the most prolific curses recorded in the Bible. We ought to ask, which response is to be emulated? What's particularly humorous is the irony of finding Job's three "friends" quoted occasionally on inspirational material, as though they were really friends—as though they spoke words of comfort—as though they spoke what was right when God explicitly states in the end that they did not. The real challenge, of course, is that their words are sometimes true, and yet the men themselves are *wrong*. Finally, Leviathan and the many other glories of creation spun through Yahweh's response to Job in the whirlwind paint exotic and stunning images. Yet, given the broader context of a man covered in boils, deprived of his children and livelihood, and pursued by accusers apparently seeking his complete destruction, one wonders whether that breathtaking photograph of the thunderstorm with a caption from Job 38 doesn't somehow sentimentalize the text, if not actually distort it by dislocating it from the original narrative.

For examples of modernism, on the other end of the spectrum, Job is torn apart by the vultures of unbelief in the academy through so-called scientific methods of "textual criticism" or straight-up philosophical denunciations. The former dissect the text into so much confetti and then reluctantly admit that a few of the scraps

# Introduction

left on the table may have some relation. Textual variants, changes in tone, linguistic texture, genre, rare vocabulary, and any number of other observations pass for excuses not to take the text seriously. On this reading, exegesis of Job (like much of scripture) is an elaborate game of *Jenga*. One wonders how much of this is evasion, an attempt at escaping responsibility for what the text actually says. Other modernists are more honest with the text, and straightforwardly condemn the God of the book of Job as capricious and negligent. They careen from accusations of stupidity and evil.

While we may locate a failure to read and appreciate the book of Job in some kind of underlying unbelief or even some form of scholarly laziness, a great deal of the problem lies in reading the Bible as a whole. For example, the themes of justice, suffering, and mercy are wound through nearly every page of Scripture. Reading all of Scripture as a united and ultimately coherent symphony of movements and alternating modes depends ultimately on a respect of the Scriptural tradition which in turn is grounded in a robust doctrine of inspiration. While recognizing a full spectrum of human texture in the words of Scripture, the Doctrine of Inspiration insists that the Holy Spirit oversaw and superintended every last word of the Bible as its primary author. In this way, the Spirit frees us to read the Bible from Genesis to Revelation, listening for the echoes, playing the various lines of "music" off one another, tuning our understanding to the harmony of the Word.

As we look at Job more closely, the parallels between Job and many other biblical characters come into focus. We will see figures like Adam and Jacob and ultimately the Lord Jesus emerging from the narrative of Job. Like a skilled composer, the author, through the working of the Spirit, weaves words, themes, and motifs from all over the Scriptures into the narrative and poetry of Job: creation and exodus, sacrifice and ritual, justice and mercy, wisdom and worship, and of course death and resurrection, all of the greatest melodies coursing down through the ages of revelation.

We should also note as we consider the book of Job that we have inspired, albeit brief, commentary on Job. Ezekiel is the only Old Testament book that refers to Job explicitly, and he lists him

## INTRODUCTION

with Noah and Daniel as the most righteous men to that point in history (Ezek. 14:14, 20). James gives us the only other explicit commentary on Job, and points in particular to Job's perseverance and the end of the story as proof of the Lord's compassion and mercy (Jas. 5:11). James says we should look to Job is an example of a prophet who spoke in the name of the Lord and endured suffering with patience (Jas. 5:10). We will return to this exhortation from James later as we consider Job the Prophet.

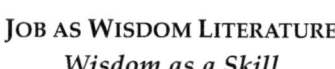

### JOB AS WISDOM LITERATURE
#### *Wisdom as a Skill*

Job is the first book in the Wisdom literature in our English Bibles. In the Hebrew Bible, it's included in what is called the Writings of Scripture, but the content and style of Job grant this book a standing with the Wisdom literature of the Bible. If that seems odd, a number of elements in the book remind us of elements that we more readily identify as Wisdom literature. Mention "Wisdom literature" and many Christians will immediately think of Proverbs or Ecclesiastes. Wisdom literature is concerned with the *meaning of life*. How does the world work? What's life all about? What's truth? What's wisdom? What's knowledge? There are a number of things in Job that are very reminiscent of Proverbs and Ecclesiastes. Of course, there is wisdom found throughout Scripture—Scripture *is* our wisdom literature in an important way—but these books in particular dwell on these subjects in a concentrated form.

One way to describe the book of Job is as an extended argument between the book of Proverbs and the book of Ecclesiastes. Proverbs generalizes about the way the world works: fools are like *this*, wise people are like *this*, you do this and you'll get blessed; you do that and you'll get in big trouble. Ecclesiastes says that the world doesn't always work that way. Sometimes you do what's right, and you still get in trouble. Sometimes that other fellow does what is wrong, and he keeps getting blessed anyway. That's in a nutshell a small version of those books, and much of the arguments in Job are concerned with these seemingly contradictory visions of life. The three friends of Job seem to be reading their cues with mathematical precision from the book of Proverbs. They have logical proofs and diagrams, and their conclusions are something reminiscent of the disciples' question to Jesus. "So who sinned, this man or his parents?" In this tidy-minded world there are only two options, and we might as well get down to brass tacks. However, Job sees through the veneer of piety in the so-called friends, sees their evil intentions, how they twist the principles of Scripture to their purposes, and at the same time he insists that the world is more complicated and challenging than they are willing to admit. In one sense, we can see Job as Proverbs and Ecclesiastes arrayed for battle.

That Job is a forty-two-chapter argument or as much a mud-wrestling throw-down as anything else, is another way of describing how Job is Wisdom Literature. In the Bible, wisdom is not theoretical. Wisdom doesn't exist in heads, to be published in arcane philosophy journals and parsed and diagrammed by men with sweater vests and pipes (no offense to my sweater-vest-wearing, pipe-smoking readers). If biblical wisdom were a vocation, it would be something like an auto mechanic or a construction worker. Wisdom is a skill, and if wisdom were a degree you would have to get it at the local Vo-Tech school. The very first use of the word "wisdom" in the Bible illustrates this point well. It is used in the book of Exodus, where Yahweh's "Spirit of wisdom" is poured out on Aholiab and Bezalel in order to equip them to design and build the tabernacle (Ex. 31:2–11; 35:30–35). Having the Spirit meant they were construction workers, architects, and artisans. It meant they knew how to pour concrete, were good with numbers, and could run a machine shop with creativity. The Spirit was poured out upon them to give them skills to build the house of God; wisdom is artistic and creative construction management. This should not come as a surprise since the first instance of the work of the Spirit in the Bible is Genesis 1, where we are told that the Spirit hovers over the waters of the primordial creation (Gen. 1:2). The Spirit is present for the very first building project in the history of the world. The Spirit empowers the Word spoken by the Father, and light bursts into the darkness, seas and dry land appear, and the stars and galaxies are flung into their whirling dances. As Peter Leithart has pointed out, the creation week is structured carefully to describe the world as a house with three stories: heaven (upstairs), earth (main level), and seas (basement).[2] When the Spirit isn't constructing one of those levels, he is filling the house with walking, swarming, creeping, and flying things. The Spirit is the Wisdom of God for laying foundations, building walls, and putting up scaffolding. Wisdom is a master craftsman (Prov. 8:30). If the wisdom of the Spirit had a uniform, it would be a hard hat, a reflective vest, and steel-toed boots.

## *Wisdom for the World*

If we stop here, we have given a very inadequate definition of wisdom. This is why the Holy Spirit inspired both Proverbs and Ecclesiastes. In other words, while it may be helpful to see the book of Job in some ways as an argument between Proverbs and Ecclesiastes, in the end we must insist that Proverbs and Ecclesiastes are actually very good friends. These books complement and explain one another. If Proverbs generally explores wisdom as a skill, Ecclesiastes explores wisdom as a very *unique* sort of skill. Wisdom is a skill, but it is both like and unlike many other skills. The famous episode at the beginning of Solomon's reign, where the new king recognizes his inability to rule the people well, illustrates this. He says that he is a "little child" and asks Yahweh God for "an understanding heart to judge" the people of Israel (1 Kings 3:7–9). The Lord is pleased with this request, answers Solomon's prayer, and immediately Solomon is confronted in the text with a test case: the two prostitutes and the baby (1 Kings 3:16ff). It may be that wisdom is a skill, a form of construction management, but behind this house-building project is always the plan to build Yahweh's house *out of people*. All the details—all the long passages describing both the construction of the tabernacle and the temple—are there because of God's great concern for his people. He cares about them,

---

2. Peter Leithart, *A House for My Name* (Moscow, ID: Canon Press, 2000).

and the building projects are meant to teach them about how they must live and love one another and work together to be his house.

If the skills needed to live and build in God's world are crucially centered on people, an entirely different sort of skill is needed than a simple, straightforward following of directions. People are messy, complicated, confusing, and frustrating. They have cultural differences, personality quirks, gifts, weaknesses, health problems, sin, and they frequently fail and let us down. People are like prostitutes fighting over a baby. In many ways, it's far easier to build a house out of bricks, wood, or stone, than to build a house out of people. At least the bricks usually stay put.

Yet the world doesn't stay put. Bricks may not have emotional meltdowns and sinful addictions or erratic, unpredictable behavior, but they do crumble and fall down eventually, and sometimes unexpectedly. Sometimes the earth doesn't sit still, and it shakes dramatically and buildings, roads, and houses collapse and break apart. Sometimes the sea doesn't stay where we left it, and it comes running up over our cities and homes, and leaves them like so many sand castles at the beach, smooth lumps of nondescript earth. Sometimes, less dramatically, it rains a bunch, or, conversely, it doesn't rain. Maybe it rains on the *wrong* day, and an entire crop, a year's worth of wages, is lost. In other words, not only are people challenging, complex, and unpredictable, but the world itself is unwieldy. This kind of wisdom comes with age and experience, being a person in this world, knowing other people, loving other people, and beginning to work through the complications and challenges and blessings of this world. Wisdom is a mantle, a crown that is given to those who begin to learn these lessons. Wisdom is kingly.

James Jordan has pointed out that in Scripture, the offices of priest, king, and prophet follow a progression of maturity and glory and generally correspond to Israel's history. The role of a priest is to guard God's house and requires strict adherence to the law. This corresponds to Israel's early history, particularly the covenant at Sinai and the ceremonial laws that attended that covenant. Priests must follow careful instructions regarding ceremonial and sacrificial law, and they may not deviate from the letter of the law. The office of king follows this, where the law must be applied with wisdom. Kings must "grow up" to wrestle with difficult issues and questions, and contemplate applications not directly addressed in the law. The kingdom era in Israel's history follows this next stage, and Solomon is a great picture of this. In order to judge between the quarreling prostitutes (1 Kings 3:16–28), the king must not only guard the law and meditate on the law (like a priest), but he must also begin to apply the law to difficult and complex situations. He must wrestle with right and wrong, light and darkness, and judge righteously. The "little child" must grow up. This kingly struggling and judging eventually grows up into the mantle of a prophet. This is the last stage in biblical maturity and glory. The prophet is one who, in his most basic role, is allowed access into the deliberations of God, the heavenly council room.

The first prophet in Scripture is Abraham who intercedes for the afflicted and is heard (Gen. 20:7, 17). He also speaks into the counsels of God regarding Sodom and Gomorrah (Gen. 18:16–33). While we see prophets throughout Scripture, they take on a particular prominence toward the end of the kingdom era in Israel's history and follow God's people down into exile. The prophet knows the law and has internalized it like a priest, has exercised wisdom as a king in making difficult judgments, and has grown up into one who has a standing to speak before God and the divine assembly and his prayers and intercessions are heard. Because the prophet has been involved in the divine deliberations, he is supremely qualified to announce those verdicts. This is why prophets frequently speak in the name of the Lord and declare his intentions and judgments; this is because they were there when it was all decided. Surely he does nothing unless he has revealed his secret to his servants the prophets (Amos 3:7).

## *The Spirit of Wisdom*

The final point to be made concerning wisdom goes back to the point we began with, which is that wisdom comes from the Spirit of God. It is the Spirit who was with God in the beginning when the foundations of the earth were laid. It is the Spirit who comes upon Bezalel and Aholiab in order to equip the artisans with creativity and skill. We ought to say that wisdom is Spiritual, except that frequently when we say that something is Spiritual, we translate that into some kind of holy speak. If we are to think and speak biblically, we ought to think of Spiritual men in the Bible like Samson and Jesus. Being "spiritual" does not mean floating about a foot off the ground or praying with a really passionate voice on Sunday morning. Spiritual simply means empowered by the Holy Spirit. The word for Spirit is the same word for breath and wind. The Spirit is the great Wind/Breath of the Father and the Son. The Spirit is the storm of God's presence—the creative, constructive, and sometimes destructive storm. This is why when the Spirit comes upon Samson, he frequently acts like a storm. Jesus is baptized by John and immediately the Spirit comes upon him and drives him into the wilderness to do battle with Satan. The Spirit drives like a wind, like a storm, and empowers men and women to carry out great deeds according to the will of the Father and the Son.

Wind is unpredictable, wild, and dangerous. Hurricanes and tornadoes don't make good pets. One does not sign peace treaties with El Niño, even if such a thing could be done. This is why thinking about wisdom as a skill is inadequate by itself. Wisdom *is* a skill. Wisdom *is* kingly judgment, but it is also difficult, dangerous, and recognizes how vaporous life, history, and the world can be. The Spirit comes and goes and blows where he wishes. The world itself is difficult and dangerous. It fades, changes, and realities can crumble overnight.

This is the key: the same Spirit who hovered over the waters of the original creation still hovers over the world, blowing and driving history forward. The same Spirit of Wisdom who created all things also rules all things, and that Spirit has been given to men. Like telling which prostitute was the true mother of the baby, wisdom requires creativity, taking chances, gut feelings, but these instincts and judgment, are not without hope, not aimless or without aid. We are promised wisdom as we ask for it, and as we follow the Spirit (Jas. 1:5). Wisdom really would be a degree from a Vo-Tech school, but classes would have to include learning skills like catching lightning, directing storms, and hang-gliding in tornadoes. What is amazing is that this is exactly what Jesus promises as we take up our cross and follow him. In Christ, the winds and storms of life becomes a path into the storm of God's presence through the power of the Spirit.

What Augustine and Gregory and many of our forefathers in the faith recognized was that this strenuous journey into the presence of God, this ascent, this sometimes jarring ride we call life is a path carved by love. The Holy Spirit is not only the Wisdom of God, but he is also the love of God, binding Father and Son together in perfect union. It was this love that anointed Jesus in his baptism and drove him into the wilderness to do battle with Satan. This love empowered him to preach the good news to the poor of Israel, enduring the mockery and rejection of his own, and it was this love that hung the Son of the Father on the cross. This Spirit of love raised the Son from the dead and raised him to glory at the right hand of the Father. It is this same love that has been poured out into our hearts in order to unite us to the Son and the Father and draw us up into his communion.

Reading and studying the book of Job is itself an introduction to this love, and to the wisdom of this love. This book is a storm of words and ideas and people, and they don't sit still quietly in their seats. They are abrupt, contradictory, and argumentative. Here, we are invited to walk with Job as priest, struggle and fight with him and his friends as kings searching for truth—searching for God— and finally we, like Job, come face-to-face with Yahweh in the whirlwind. For those who have ears to hear and eyes to see, Job is a powerful invitation to grow up into maturity, patience, and holiness through struggle, trial, argument, and prayer, looking for the glory of the resurrection in the power and love of the Holy Spirit.

## Date and Author

Who was Job? Who wrote Job? When? These are questions that have been asked for centuries without conclusive or certain answers. The book itself is anonymous and does not leave many clues for the careful student. Since the early Church, speculation has varied widely, suggesting Moses, Job, Elihu, Solomon, or one of the other prophets as the author. Job certainly sounds like he's from the era of the patriarchs. He has lots of children and cattle and dies full of days like a patriarch. It would not be strange to find out that Job was a contemporary of Abraham or Jacob, and there is some precedent for this view. According to the Septuagint, the Greek translation of the Old Testament, Job was an Edomite, descended from Esau and that same Jobab who is mentioned in Genesis 35:33 and 36:34. The Septuagint appends the last verse of Job with the following paragraph of additional information.

> And it is written that he will rise again with those whom the Lord raises up. This man is described in the Syriac book *as* living in the land of Ausis, on the borders of Idumea and Arabia: and his name before was Jobab; and having taken an Arabian wife, he begot a son whose name was Ennon. And he himself was the son of his father Zare, one of the sons of Esau, and of his mother Bosorrha, so that he was the fifth from Abraam. And these were the kings who reigned in Edom, which country he also ruled over: first, Balac, the son of Beor, and the name of his city was Dennaba: but after Balac, Jobab, who is called Job, and after him Asom, who was governor out of the country of Thaeman: and after him Adad, the son of Barad, who destroyed Madiam in the plain of Moab; and the name of his city was Gethaim. And *his* friends who came to him were Eliphaz, of the children of Esau, king of the Thaemanites, Baldad son of the Sauchaeans, Sophar king of the Minaeans.

Given that Job echoes many of the same themes of Wisdom Literature, it seems reasonable to suggest that Solomon or another wise man from the early Kingdom era composed or compiled the final version of the book of Job. Others have suggested Hezekiah as another possible author. Even if the work is of several different pieces compiled by a final author or redactor, this hardly denigrates its meaning or place in Holy Scripture. The Spirit is fond of adventures, suspense, and close calls, and it would certainly not be beyond or above him to implicate the hands of several in the final product of his purpose. However, there are good reasons simply to assume a single author.

If we are to take the work of the Spirit seriously, this means paying attention to all the details. Inspiration ought not to mean that we may merely skim the text of Scripture, running the sandpaper of our preconceived notions over the fine print to make it smooth and happy for our confessions of faith. Contrary to our urge to skim or glance, inspiration authorizes and compels us to pay attention to the words, the spelling, the nuances, the parallels, and all the music in the text. What we find in Job is that much of the language is unique, with many words not occuring anywhere else in the Old Testament. Particularly in the middle poetic section of the dialogues, simply on the basis of vocabulary, many believe that Job must be the product of a later author. We have no other records of vocabulary like this from the early Kingdom era. A number of commentators have also suggested that it was originally in Aramaic or some similar language. They suggest that the final form we have is actually a translation, and in some cases, a *transliteration* into Hebrew.

In fact, I am told that among some Hebrew scholars the joke is as follows: in most of the Hebrew Scriptures, the great task of translation and scholarship is investigating how paragraphs cohere, following the train of thought carefully, and understanding the context. In most Hebrew *poetry*, the great task is narrowed to figuring out how words in a particular line or sentence relate and unite to create a coherent thought. However, when it comes to Joban scholarship, we are sometimes reduced to trying to figure out how one Hebrew letter relates to another![3]

None of this should worry us. If the book of Job is one of the greatest literary masterpieces of the Hebrew Bible, why would we be surprised to find such linguistic mastery, such poetic expansiveness? The same Spirit that inspires God-breathed leaves and sunsets and raindrops, all one-by-one, was free to do the same with every word, every letter he sang into the Scriptures. It is the glory

---

3. Thanks to Ben Merkle for this.

of God to conceal many matters, and it is the glory of kings to search them out.

## STRUCTURE, STYLE, AND CHARACTERS

While we do not know for sure who Job was, it seems reasonable to follow the Septuagint tradition in identifying Job as a descendent of Esau, one of the great Edomite kings.[4] Other views include the idea that Job was himself a mere legend, a mythological or parabolic character, but the references in Ezekiel and James to Job assume that Job was a real, historical figure. We have no good reason to doubt this. As an Edomite king, Job was a Gentile, outside of the covenant people of God. While Job's wife remains nameless, Job's three daughters are named in the epilogue: Jemimah, Keziah, and Keren-Happuch, apparently meaning Dove, Cinnamon, and Horn-of-Eye-Shadow.[5]

The name *Iyob* has various possibilities for translation. One suggestion for the meaning of the name Job is "Where is my father?" It may also be a pun on the word for "enemy," and Job may be playing off this when he says that he is an "enemy" of God (13:24).

The book of Job is structured by five basic sections with varying lengths. The book opens with a short prologue (1–2) and closes with an epilogue (42:7ff). These sections are stylistically very similar, told in simple, almost fairy tale-like prose. Characters are larger than life, time is nearly suspended; there are many repeated phrases, titles, and symbols that play important roles. There is a cosmic yet familial and patriarchal feel to these sections as the narrator gives up-close snapshots of Job's seemingly idyllic family and estate, but at the same time draws back the curtain into heaven where God holds counsel with the sons of God. These two bookends hold together the bulk of the book which begins with Job's great curse and lament in chapter 3 and is followed by twenty-seven more chapters of dialogue

---

4. See James B. Jordan, "Was Job an Edomite King?" Biblical Horizons No. 130 (http://www.biblicalhorizons.com/biblical-horizons/130/).

5. Ellen Davis suggests these translations in her essay "Job and Jacob" in *The Whirlwind*, ed., Stephen L. Cook (New York: Sheffield Academic Press, 2001), 120.

between Job and his three friends: Eliphaz, Bildad, and Zophar. This dialogue follows a cyclical pattern of Job speaking, being responded to by each friend, and Job responding to each in turn: Job, Eliphaz, Job, Bildad, Job, Zophar, Job. This cycle grows up into a fierce debate which degenerates midway through the third cycle (seemingly cutting Bildad's third speech short and lacking a third response from Zophar), and Job's words are finally ended in chapter 31. These dialogues sound and feel very different from the prologue and epilogue. In contrast, these dialogues are only speech, and therefore have no description of the world around the speakers. Instead of an omniscient narrator giving sweeping descriptions, we have a very narrow universe centered on the words of these four men. The content of their words gropes and struggles for cosmic, universal truth and justice, but it is tentative and contested. Where all is black and white (for better or worse) in the legendary style of the prologue and epilogue, all is misty, foggy, and vaporous in the dialogues.

A fourth character emerges in chapter 32, a young man named Elihu who gives a lengthy response to Job and the three friends. His style is very similar to the other characters, but his role in the dialogue is not clear and frequently contested. Elihu gives more of a monologue and is not clearly a true participant in the dialogue. Finally, in chapter 38, Yahweh answers Job out of the whirlwind in two or three consecutive speeches to which Job gives short responses. The style here is different yet again in the sweeping imagery and poetry of Yahweh's questioning of Job. Yet, there is something of the dialogue form still in play even if the speeches of Yahweh clearly dominate. We will keep this structure and these stylistic textures in mind as we work through the text.

    I. Prologue (1–2)
    II. Dialogues (3–31)
    III. Elihu (32–37)
    IV. Yahweh (38–42:6)
    V. Epilogue (42:7–17)

# Part One

# The Prologue

## 2

## ADAM AND SONS: JOB 1:1–5

"Once upon a time, in a land far, far away, there lived a king who had seven sons and three daughters." The book of Job opens in the simplicity and beauty of a fairy tale.

Job is introduced as a man from the land of Uz who was "blameless and upright, one who feared God and turned away from evil" (1:1). Job is a perfect man, an Adam in an Eden-garden. Job is described as "blameless" like Noah (Gen. 6:9), Jacob (Gen. 25:27), and David (1 Kings 9:4). This is the same word used to describe those animals to be offered as sacrifices. They must be "perfect" or "without blemish" (Ex. 12:5; Lev. 1:3). This is the standard to which Abraham is urged by the Lord (Gen. 17:1) and refers not to a state of sinless perfection but integrity, honesty, and loyalty to God.

To be "upright" means listening to the voice of Yahweh, obeying his laws carefully (Ex. 15:26; Deut. 12:28; 1 Kings 9:4), and imitating Yahweh himself (Deut. 32:4). The word is also associated with that which is pleasing or satisfying (Judges 14:3, 7; 1 Sam. 18:20), and in that sense can describe being ruled by personal desires and opinions (Judges 17:6; 21:25) in contrast to the righteous rulers commended in the book of Kings for doing what is "right in the eyes of the Lord" (1 Kings 11:38; 15:11; 2 Kings 10:30).

The titles of "blameless and upright" are also explained in the verses that follow. Job is blameless and upright specifically in so far as he "feared God and turned away from evil." This is nearly a direct quote from several passages describing the way of wisdom in Proverbs (3:7; 8:13; 16:6). In the first verse of the book, Job is identified as a man who embodies wisdom, discernment, and righteous rule, an Adam who images God faithfully.

Not only is Job a *faithful* Adam, he is also immediately described as a *fruitful* Adam. Job has been fruitful and has multiplied. He has seven sons and three daughters. His possessions are great: seven thousand sheep, three thousand camels, five hundred yoke of oxen, and five hundred female donkeys (1:2). Job is an Adam-like king who rules over creation. God created man in his image and said, "Be fruitful and multiply and fill the earth and subdue it and have dominion over the fish of the sea and over the birds of the heavens and over every living thing that moves on the earth" (Gen. 1:28). Job has done that; he has been fruitful and multiplied, and he rules over the beasts of the field and rules over them well. He's an Adam in his kingdom.

All of the numbers used underline Job's faithfulness and fruitfulness. The text tells us in relative detail that he has seven sons and three daughters, seven thousand sheep and three thousand camels (two sets of sevens and threes), and five hundred yoke of oxen and five hundred female donkeys (a set of five and five). All of the numbers add up to ten, which is a number associated with fullness and abundance. Rebekah is blessed by her brothers who pray that she would be the mother of "ten thousands" (Gen. 24:60), Joseph sends word to his father Israel that he is alive, accompanied by "ten donkeys loaded with the good things of Egypt and ten female donkeys loaded with grain, bread, and provision" (Gen. 45:23). We might also note the number of tens in the construction of the tabernacle (Ex. 26:1, 16; 27:12), the fact that God gives ten commandments (Ex. 20:1–17; 34:28), and later Elkanah will liken his faithfulness and provision for Hannah to the blessing of ten sons (1 Sam. 1:8). The number ten also symbolizes fullness of judgment and destruction: it is with ten plagues that God strikes the land of Egypt.

Job is also called the greatest of all the people of the east (1:3). Like the garden which was planted in the east of Eden, Job lives in a great garden in the east. Job is an Adam, a great king. We don't know exactly where he was from, or where Uz was located, but it seems consistent with an area of Edom (cf. Gen. 36:28; Lam. 4:21).

This location is even related to Job's character. If Job is an Adam, he is also a glorified Adam, a wise and fruitful king like Solomon. The land of the east by the time of Solomon was known for its wisdom and knowledge. Solomon's own wisdom is described as surpassing even the wisdom of the people of the east (1 Kings 4:30). Literally, in both Job 1:3 and 1 Kings 4:30, the phrase is "all the sons of the east." While most Bibles translate this as "people" or "children," it is significant that Job is referred to specifically as a "son." Job, like Solomon, is presented as one who has heeded his father's instruction. He has listened to the wise lessons and proverbs of his father (Prov. 1:8; 2:1; 3:1). His prosperity and blessing are not accidental; they are the result of obeying his father. In this sense, we can say that "Job's journey begins, in effect, where the book of Proverbs ends."[1] We will consider more of the significance of this status of "son" in the following chapter, but it should be noted at this point that Job is a son-king like Adam, a *wise* son-king like Solomon (cf. 1 Kings 4:20–34).

The feasts of Job's sons and daughters also fit with these Edenic and Solomonic themes. Part of Adam's job was to try out the

---

1. William P. Brown, *Character in Crisis: A Fresh Approach to the Wisdom Literature of the Old Testament* (Grand Rapids, MI: Eerdmans, 1996), 51.

strawberries and the blueberries, enjoy and cultivate the produce, all the good food that God had created. Adam's job was to rule and feast, and Solomon's reign glimpsed something of this glory. His provisions for one day are enormous, and all who come to King Solomon's table are filled (1 Kings 4:22–23, 27). Job's sons are princes who are beginning to share in this rule and feasting. Job's sons' and daughters' feasting is another sign of Job's prosperity, glory, and blessing, but it is also a sign of his Solomonic wisdom and diligence in taking dominion.

While these may be any number of different sorts of feasts, the specific designation "each on his own day" may refer specifically to birthdays. In chapter 3, Job unleashes a curse on "his own day," referring specifically to the day of his birth. Regardless, the text suggests a couple of sevens in regard to the feasts and subsequent sacrifices of Job on their behalf. If each son hosts a feast on "his own day," this amounts to seven feasts in a given year. Job is also said to have offered sacrifices according to the "number of them all" which likewise would seem to be seven.[2] These sevens underline a Sabbath theme in these early verses of Job. Job and his household enjoy Sabbath rest in their feasting and worship. Their entire world is balanced and peaceful. Their world is "very good."

## JOB AND HIS SONS

Job's integrity and righteousness is also evidenced in his care for his children. He loves them. He is concerned for them, and so even in the days of their feasting and their rejoicing before the Lord, Job sends and sanctifies them, and the text says he would rise early in the morning and offer burnt offerings according to the number of them all. There are several things to notice here.

First, this introduces a key theme in the book of Job, the theme of "cursing" God. Job said, "It may be that my sons have sinned and cursed God in their hearts." In fact, the text famously says, "It

---

2. Perhaps if these seven sacrifices were offered after each of the seven feasts, this suggests a total of forty-nine annual sacrifices.

may be that my sons have sinned and *blessed* God in their hearts." The word for "cursed" is the word *barak*, the usual word for "bless," but it is used here in an apparently euphemistic way to mean "curse." Later in the same chapter, the Satan[3] will say that Job only fears Yahweh because he has "*blessed* the work of his hands" (1:10). This is the same word and used in its ordinary sense. However, in the verse following, the Satan urges Yahweh to stretch out his hand against Job, "and he will surely *curse* you to your face" (1:11). Again, here the word is the usual word for "bless," used euphemistically. This word continues to be used in these opposing senses throughout the prologue. Ironically, Job does "bless" Yahweh after he is struck, saying, "blessed be the name of Yahweh" (1:21), but he clearly means "bless" in its traditional sense. Nevertheless, the Satan urges Yahweh to touch Job's bones and flesh promising that Job really will "curse you to your face," again using the word "bless" in this unusual way. Finally, Job's wife mimics the Satan by urging Job to "curse God and die," wielding the word "bless" as curse. The word is used only two more times in the rest of the book and both times in its ordinary meaning. Outside of Job, the word is only used this way in a couple of places.

In 1 Kings 21, the word is used in the story of Naboth's vineyard. The two false witnesses, the "sons of Belial," accuse Naboth of "cursing" God and the king (1 Kings 21:10, 13). The word is *barak*, but it clearly means to denounce, blaspheme, or curse God and the king, because the recommendation (and result) is to stone Naboth for his alleged crime. Another possible instance of this sort of usage is in Psalm 10:3. The wording is more ambiguous, but clearly the psalmist is identifying someone who is wicked. Some translations render the word *barak* as curse and direct it specifically at Yahweh. The King James Version says that this person "blesseth the covetous," but either way the "blessing" here is used to describe a cumulative curse, whether directly or indirectly. To bless the covetous is to spit in the face of God.

---

3. The Hebrew text literally spells Satan's names as "The Satan," and we frequently follow suit. More on this below.

While this usage of the word "bless" may strike us as strange and even a bit troubling (e.g., "How could a word mean the opposite of its usual meaning?"), a moment's reflection reveals that languages are not averse to this sort of thing. Consider the word "good." With a bit of sarcasm or irony, it takes very little to flip the meaning of this word inside out. A wife announces that she has burned dinner, and a husband responds "Oh, good!" Consider this word used in farewell rituals: we say "goodbye" to loved ones and relatives and dear friends, and the same "blessing" can be flung at unwanted solicitors, treacherous friends, or unfaithful lovers. "Goodbye" (while still indicating a kind of farewell) can bend in on itself and the "good" is the departure.

Others have noted a similar parallel in Hebrew usage. *Barak* functions as a farewell blessing in some contexts (Gen. 31:55; Josh. 22:6), and it has been suggested that this is the root of the usage in Job.[4] To bid farewell can easily amount to a curse, as we have just seen. To bid farewell to God, for instance, would be to curse God.

On a more global theological level, part of the question being pondered by the book of Job is whether blessing is really *blessing*. Job wonders if his sons have blessed/cursed God in their hearts while feasting and enjoying the blessings of God. The Satan insists that when God removes the hedge of protection, Job will bless/curse God to his face, again suggesting that Job's blessing of God is superficial and contingent on prosperity. That blessing, the Satan contends, will in actuality be cursing if God allows Job to be struck. The answer to these questions is found in the refusal of Job to actually curse God. While Job will vigorously argue with God and curse a great deal about his life and circumstances, Job does not in fact curse God. Finally, the epilogue is the emphatic answer to this verbal question. In the end God "blesses" Job even more than he was blessed at the beginning (42:12). Even apart from the exact numbers and nature of the blessing, the linguistic point is

---

4. William Henry Green, *Conflict and Triumph* (Carlisle, PA: The Banner of Truth Trust, 1999), 12.

underlined. God's blessing really is *blessing*. While Satan sought to turn blessing into cursing, God turns that attempted curse back into blessing.

Carol Newsom also points out that part of this play on words results in there being (literally) no curses in the prologue or epilogue.[5] No character is allowed to curse, or even say the word "curse." As we have noted, ultimately the "cursing" is turned to blessing, but this is already retroactively applied to the words of the speakers. They mean to say "curse" but "bless" is all that comes out! Blessing is underwritten or superimposed into the text. As Joseph explains to his brothers, what they meant for evil, God meant for good (Gen. 50:20). God's meaning always penetrates every event, every intention without failure.

One last comment on this usage: while we ordinarily praise Job for his piety toward his sons, there is perhaps something of doubt or fear in Job's actions as well. Without completely undermining Job's actions—they are presented as part of Job's integrity—Job himself later recognizes that he was living in fear and dread of calamity (3:25). His actions toward his children were pious but also motivated and tinged with some uncertainty.[6] That of which Job was uncertain is explicit and vicious accusation in the Satan before Yahweh. The Satan roams the earth accusing men, assuming their frailty and weakness, seeing them as inclined to "curse God." Job is not of course *accusing* his sons directly, but the parallel is still present. He is "going to and fro" considering the state of his own household and his children in particular. The contrast is that Job is not an accuser but a mediator and priest, an advocate for his sons. If Job has a similar perspective, Job does not have the same role in the least. Job recognizes possible weakness and offers sacrifices, but the Satan recognizes possible weakness and urges God to remove the hedge of protection and blessing. On the other hand, we might

---

5. Carol A. Newsom, *The Book of Job: A Contest of Moral Imaginations* (Oxford: Oxford University Press, 2003), 55.

6. Stephen L. Cook, Corrine L. Patton, and James W. Watts, eds. *The Whirlwind: Essays on Job, Hermeneutics and Theology in Memory of Jane Morse*, 120.

also draw this parallel even more strongly between Yahweh and Job. Job is a faithful father who seeks the blessing of his sons to the point of even offering sacrifices to protect them from unintentional sins. This is almost identical to the accusation that the Satan levels at Yahweh. The Satan will accuse Yahweh of putting a hedge of protection around Job and seems to accuse Yahweh of being a "hovering Father"[7] constantly watching out for his son Job, just as Job does for his sons. There will be more on this parallel later.

### Faithful Father

Another key to understanding what Job is doing for his children is embedded in the theology of sacrifice in the Old Testament. The word here and throughout the Old Testament translated "burnt offerings" would be better translated as "ascension" offering. The word doesn't mean burnt—it means "to go up."[8] Literally, he would get up early in the morning, and he would cause to go up *ascensions*. The offering is called an Ascension Offering or a going-up offering because the animal is turned into smoke and goes up. The priest would cut the animal into particular pieces, arrange it on the altar, and light it on fire, turning the animal into smoke and causing the animal to ascend in smoke to the Lord. The smoke rises to God, and, as Leviticus repeatedly says, it is a soothing aroma to him. This is how a worshipper might draw near to Yahweh and be considered acceptable in his sight (Lev. 1).

The focus of that particular offering is on burning the animal so that the smoke rises into the presence of God. The symbolism and the theology behind the Ascension Offering is communion with God in heaven, and *you* can't get there. You have to have a substitute. So an Israelite would take an animal as a substitute, laying his hands on

---

7. Brown, *Character in Crisis*, 53.
8. See, for exmple, James B. Jordan, *The Whole Burnt Sacrifice: Its Liturgy and Meaning*, Biblical Horizons Occasional Papers No. 11 (Biblical Horizons: Niceville, FL, 1991), or Jeffrey J. Meyers, *The Lord's Service* (Moscow, ID: Canon Press, 2003).

it and saying "this is me," and then cut it up, put it on the altar, and watch the animal go up to the presence of God in smoke.

Job is an Adam, but we remember that Adam sinned. He was exiled from the Garden to the east, and cherubim were stationed at the entrance of the east side of the Garden so that he could not get back to the Tree of Life (Gen. 3:24). That means in order to get back into the presence and fellowship of God, he was going to have to go through those cherubim. Those cherubim have a great, flaming sword, and he was going to have to go through the sword and fire. One must be cut up and transformed by fire in order to get back into the presence and fellowship of God.

The same thing is symbolized in all of the sacrifices while highlighting other aspects of reconciliation and forgiveness, but the Ascension Offering dwells on these themes in particular. Job offers these sacrifices for his sons regularly. He is concerned that his sons may have sinned and cursed God in their hearts.

Frequently, we think of sin as only a ledger: God's record of all our evil thoughts, words, and actions versus our good thoughts, words, and actions. Sin is imagined as a substance that builds up in our system, in our account. Perhaps there may be helpful analogies there, but sin is also a directional thing, a geographical reality, a sort of teleology. Literally, the verb in the Hebrew "to sin" means "to miss the mark"; it means you've veered off the path. To sin is to be going in the wrong direction, to be in the wrong place.

So what does Job do? Job is saying, God, I'm not sure what my sons have been doing, but I want to reorient them to you again. I'm not sure where they've been, I'm not sure what they've said. I'm not sure what's going on in their hearts, so I'm offering them back to you again. This one is for my firstborn, this one is for my secondborn, this one is for my thirdborn, and I am offering them up to you. I remind you of them. Consider my sons, and draw them into your presence. Job offers these Ascension Offerings, these sacrifices according to the number of them all, for each of his sons. Job did this regularly.

## Conclusion

As we have seen, the book of Job opens like a fairy tale in a beautiful garden. Job is an Adam who has been faithful and fruitful, and the blessing of God is all around him. Job is blameless and fears the Lord, and this wisdom has exalted Job to rule like Solomon over a great kingdom. He is the greatest of all the sons of the east. And not only is Job a faithful and wise son, but Job's children are growing up in this blessing, feasting and rejoicing in the wisdom of their faithful father whose diligence and love and care is thorough and careful.

The book of Job begins in the blessing of Proverbs, fathers and sons living faithfully and in the abundance and glory of wisdom. Yet even Proverbs self-consciously recognizes that it is only the "beginning of wisdom." Proverbs is wisdom for young men, for sons growing up, but it is not the end of wisdom, nor is it all there is to be said about wisdom. Proverbs 1 begins with the preamble intending to begin training in "wise dealing, in righteousness, justice, and equity; to give prudence to the simple, knowledge and discretion to the youth" (Prov. 1:3–4), but this is so that even the wise will hear and "increase in learning" and that "one who understands" may "obtain guidance" (Prov. 1:5). Solomon says that Proverbs is the elementary school of wisdom; it is preparatory wisdom. The hope of Solomon is that having trained in this proverbial wisdom, the wise son who understands may be prepared to "understand a proverb and a saying, the words of the wise and their riddles" (Prov. 1:6). Proverbs is training for grappling with the hard sayings, riddles, and the words of the wise. Proverbs is the foundation of the Spirit's wisdom, preparing wise sons to increase in learning, to increase in glory.

3

FATHERS, SONS, AND THE SATAN: JOB 1:6–12

The book of Job opens with fathers and sons in the family of Job, and this theme continues through the rest of the book. The father-son relationship is unique for its joys and challenges, and notorious for when it goes sour. Famous duos would include Noah and Ham, Abraham and Isaac, Jacob and Joseph, David and Absalom, Laius and Oedipus, even Darth Vader and Luke Skywalker. The relationship holds within its furnace the capacity for both tremendous blessing and horrific cursing. This volatility is tied to the fact that foundational to all human relationships is the relationship of the eternal Father and the eternal Son bound together in the love and fellowship of the eternal Spirit. This Trinitarian life is life itself, and therefore when it is bestowed in human relationships, it is all-glorious and noble and wonderful. When sin and folly abound, however, the explosions and pain are always devastating.

Yet, it is this basic understanding of fellowship, blessing, and cursing that seems horribly wrong in what follows in the story of Job. The book opens with a faithful father and his sons, a family and kingdom which seem to be overflowing in blessing, but it is this tremendous blessing and wisdom that stands juxtaposed to what follows. As the narrator draws the curtain of heaven aside and we glimpse a scene in the heavenly courtroom, readers are struck with the presence of the Satan, God's strange, even troubling interaction with the Satan, and on top of those concerns, it is reasonable to wonder why Job is not privy to this council. When God is about to do something big that effects his people, he typically announces it before hand (Gen. 18:17–18; Ex. 33:1–11; cf. Amos 3:7). Not only does God plan a great tragedy without consulting his servant Job, the tragedy is to befall Job at the instigation of the Satan. Where was Job? Why has God listened to Satan? Are there no others among the divine assembly to speak up on Job's behalf? Is this just?

## THE SONS OF GOD

The text says, "Now there was a day when the sons of God came to present themselves before Yahweh, and Satan also came in among them" (1:6). First, we need to consider what is meant by the title "sons of God." This is actually very central to what the book of Job is all about. It is not accidental that the prologue has already spoken of "sons" in four of the first five verses of the book. The author could only draw more attention to this theme if he underlined the word every time it occurred.

The title "son of God" takes us all the way back to Adam. The first son of God was Adam. Usually, conservative, Bible-believing Christians are quick to say "Son of God" means Jesus. Many faithful parents teach their children from the earliest days that Jesus is the Son of God. And of course this is true! Jesus *is* the Son of God. Jesus *is* the second person of the Trinity, the eternal Son begotten of his Father before all worlds, as the creed rightly insists. But Jesus is not the only "son of God" in the Bible, and if we are Bible-believing Christians, we want all of the Bible to inform our faith. All of the gospels are concerned with seeing that Jesus is the Son of God, but it is important to see that what the council of Nicea and the council of Chalcedon eventually defined is the culmination of a several-thousand-year story.

The story begins in the beginning with Adam. We know this from Genesis 1, because it tells us that God made Adam in his own image and in his likeness (Gen. 1:27). How do we know that Adam was the son of God? Because the text says that he *looked* like God. You know that children belong to their parents because they look like them. That's a "Smith," a "Johnson," a "Sumpter," no doubt. There's a family resemblance. That's how we know who they belong to. God created us in his image, so that we look like him. God said "let us make man in our own image, in our likeness, so that they look like us, so that they may image God in the world." That's how we know Adam was the first son of God.

Luke states this explicitly, beginning with Jesus and counting all the way back in time through the fathers: "Jesus, when he began his ministry, was about thirty years of age, being the son (as was supposed) of Joseph, the son of Heli, the son of Matthat . . . the son of Enos, the son of Seth, the son of Adam, the son of God" (Luke 3:38). It begins with Jesus and goes all the way back to Adam—Adam, the son of God. Adam was the first son of God. This means that Seth was the second son of God. Jesus is the culmination of a long line of sons of God. Luke knows this because the genealogy comes as the preface to the temptation of Jesus in the wilderness by the Devil whose questions begin and end with "if you are the Son of God" (Luke 4:3, 9). Jesus' triumph over the Devil is confirmation of what Luke saw in the genealogy of Christ. Jesus truly is the Son of God, but we have to understand the whole story of the sons of God in order to fully appreciate what Luke is doing.

Genesis 5 is worth looking at carefully on this point. We know the middle of chapter 1 well, but chapter 5 tells us again explicitly: "This is the book of the genealogy of Adam in the day that God made man. He made him in the likeness of God" (Gen. 5:1). This was already stated in 1:27, but because it is important, Moses repeats it. "He created them male and female and blessed them and called them mankind in the day that they were created. And Adam lived 130 years and begot a son in his own likeness, after his image, and named him Seth." So Seth was born in the image and likeness of Adam, who was made in the image and likeness of God. This means that Adam was the first son of God, and as has already been suggested, Seth was the second son of God. He has the same likeness and image. He represents God in the world too. This point is implicit through the rest of the genealogy. The formula is familiar: "After he begot Seth, the days of Adam were eight hundred years; and he had sons and daughters. So all the days that Adam lived were nine hundred and thirty years; and he died. Seth lived a hundred and five years and begot Enosh, after he begot Enosh, Seth lived eight hundred and seven years." The text doesn't come out and say "and Enosh was made in the image and likeness of Seth," but the formula has been established. Adam in the image and likeness of God, Seth in the image and likeness of Adam; and the reader knows the formula. Cainan, Mahalalel, Jared, each in the image and likeness of his dad, who is in the image and likeness of his dad, who is in the image and likeness of Adam, who is in the image and likeness of God. These are the first sons of God.

Adam was created with the calling to rule and to exercise dominion over the kingdom of God. God created a universe, and placed Adam in a palace-garden in the center and called him to begin ruling as prince over the kingdom. Adam, as God's created son, was created and called to rule and glorify his Father's house. Sin, however, interrupted this calling. Adam's disobedience as a son meant that he had to leave his Father's house, that there was distance now between the Father and Adam. The relationship was not obliterated, but it was broken and severely strained. Yet God was a faithful Father and promised that Adam and his sons would one day be welcome in the Father's house again. A son would come who would defeat sin and Satan, and lead all the exiled sons back home. Therefore God promised a "seed," and this seed is the genealogical line that is traced in Genesis 5 and 10. This genealogical line is the genealogy of the "sons of God" which Luke finally traces in its entirety, reveling in the arrival of Jesus at long last.

In Genesis 5, there are "other sons and daughters," and it is reasonable to point out that they too were "made in the image and likeness of God." The particular designation of the image and likeness of God has a more specific purpose. To be the "son of God" in this specific way is to take on the Father's mission in the world in a particular way, specifically to carry on the *promises* of God. All of humanity is made in the image and likeness of God and is called to bear that image *generally*. Throughout the Old Testament, the sons of God carry with them, embody, and memorialize the promises of God and the central promise of the seed who will come and defeat the serpent (Gen. 3:15).

The importance of that promised seed is emphasized in these genealogies in Genesis 5 and later in Genesis 10. This is the family line of particular individuals—sons of God who image that mission and promise of God. These genealogies are evidence and proof that God is going to come and renew his people. God is keeping his promises. This promise is fulfilled and emphasized in the patriarchs, particularly in the great tension with Abraham and Sarah's barrenness. Where is the son? Where is the heir that God has promised? These are the great questions that haunt the Abrahamic narratives, and are even more forcefully understood as: where is the next son of God? Where is the promised one who will carry on the mission and calling of the Father in the world? When Isaac is born, he is the "son of promise." He is the son who is going to carry that mission, and Jacob and his sons will grow into the nation of Israel as the son of God.

In Exodus 4, when Moses is standing at the burning bush, he is commissioned to go back to demand the release of the people of Israel. The very last thing God tells him is: "Israel is my son, my firstborn son, let him go and if you do not let my son go, I will kill *your* firstborn son" (Ex. 4:22–23). The summary of Moses' mission is God, the Father of Israel, demanding the release of his son, his people. The whole story of the Exodus, the whole story of the freeing of Israel from bondage in Egypt, is predicated on this point.

Israel is the firstborn son of God. "And if you don't let my son go," God says, "I'm going to kill your firstborn son." Of course that's what happens. There are a number of preliminaries (the first nine plagues), but Pharaoh doesn't get it and God kills Pharaoh's son, just as he promised.

Israel was called to image God as a whole, called to be his son in the world, carrying on the mission of his Father. All of the elements of the Mosaic covenant are part of this calling: the Law, the tabernacle, the holiness code, and the sacrificial service are Israel's training in bearing the image of God. However, the promise is not only for Israel. The promise is also for all the nations—all the lost and exiled sons. Israel is the son who carries on the mission of the Father in the world. Israel, as a kingdom of priests, is a memorial of the Father's house, a reminder of his promises, and many opportunities to practice and begin ministry in the Father's house again.

The title "firstborn son" underlines this vocational aspect in particular. The Old Testament practice of fathers bestowing a "double portion," or birthright of inheritance, on the firstborn son is bound up with God's original promise to the line of the promised seed. Deuteronomy guards this requirement in the law, protecting the rights of the firstborn son even of an unloved wife (Deut. 21:17). This double portion was not just a lucky gift for the firstborn (too bad for the others). Rather, the double-portion inheritance was the means by which the firstborn son was empowered to take up the calling of his father's house and mission in the world. This would include the practical needs of his father's house but also the capital needed to expand and grow that house in the world. The firstborn son was expected to take up the vocation of his father, and the double portion was the means to accomplish this task.

When Yahweh calls the nation of Israel his "firstborn son," it is not merely a term of affection or loyalty, it is also a vocational title. The firstborn son is called to serve his father and carry on his father's house. This becomes more explicit in Israel after the Passover. The Passover itself focuses on the firstborn as the firstborn of Israel are protected by the blood of the lamb on their doors while all of the firstborn of Egypt are struck down. Exodus 13 explains that when Yahweh passed through Egypt and killed the firstborn, he simultaneously claimed all the firstborn of Israel. Therefore, the firstborn of Israel must be redeemed (Ex. 34:19–20). However, instead of all the firstborn among the "sons of Israel," Yahweh takes the tribe of Levi, and he explains that this goes back to Passover (Num. 3:12–13; 8:16–18). Not only does Exodus climax in the building of Yahweh's house (the tabernacle), but the Levites are appointed as the tribe that is given specific responsibility for carrying out the operations of Yahweh's house. They represent the firstborn of Israel who in turn stand in for the entire nation of Israel as the "firstborn son" of Yahweh God. Their "double portion" is the inheritance of the house of Yahweh, the tithes and the sacrifices (Num. 18:21–26). Israel is the firstborn son of God freed from slavery in order to build his Father's house, and the Levites serve as sons in the house of God their Father, teaching all of Israel how they too are to be the son of God, embodying the promise and carrying out the mission of their Father's house in the world.

In 2 Samuel, the theme is applied to Solomon, the son of David. Yahweh says that he will make Solomon his son (2 Sam. 7:14). David has suggested that he build a house for Yahweh, and Yahweh has responded by saying that *he* will build a house for David. In this context, Yahweh says that he will set this "seed" on David's throne, and Yahweh will be his Father and he will be his son. This son will build Yahweh's house. Yahweh is the great King, and his son is his prince. The son of God builds the house of God his Father and carries on the mission of that royal house in the world. In other words, the son of God is an Adam-like king. If Adam was created to be God's reigning son on this earth, Solomon pictures that glory and power in a dim yet helpful way; however, even Solomon's glory yearns for more glory.

Not only are the "sons of God" the line of the promised seed and Israel as the chosen nation, but angels in some sense also take up this role as well. Recall that after the Fall, it was not human beings who guarded the presence of God but angels. Cherubim guard the way to the Tree of Life with a flaming sword, which the sacrificial system would constantly memorialize for Israel. The tabernacle (and later the temple) reminds Israel of this too. Israel was granted a special status and invited to draw near to Yahweh as his beloved son, but this access was still heavily guarded. Cherubim continued to guard the Most Holy Place throughout the sojourns of Israel (Ex. 25:18–22; 26:1; 1 Kings 6:23–35; 7:29).

Psalm 8 describes the place of man as a "little lower than the angels" and in the context of Genesis 3 and the rest of the Old Testament narrative, it seems fairly clear that angels take on some of the roles that Adam and his descendents were to have taken up themselves. While it appears likely that Adam was created in a kind of perfect immaturity, which probably would have included some training and teaching from the angels, Adam's sin plunges him and his descendents into a great and horrific remedial program. Later in Yahweh's answer to Job, he references the "sons of God" who shouted for joy during the week of creation, and this clearly refers to angels (Job 39:6–7). The angels helped in the creation of the world, and they would have made excellent assistants and counselors as Adam and his sons learned to rule the world in wisdom. However, the curse on Adam's sin is a great demotion, and man is put under angelic tutors (cf. Gal. 4:1–3). Angels take on many of Adam's tasks until Adam is forgiven, until he grows up into a son.[1]

In this sense, Adam and his descendants are being trained and taught to grow up into the maturity, glory, and calling which angels temporarily held. Angels represent to some extent a lost glory and authority as they guard and serve the God of heaven. Jesus seems to hint at something of the eschatological role of angelic beings when he says that humans will be like them in the resurrection, not being married or given in marriage (Matt. 22:30). Likewise, in Daniel 3, Nebuchadnezzar sees a fourth figure in the fiery furnace, one who is like the "son of the gods." Whether this is an angelic being or a theophany of the second person of the Trinity,

---

[1]. I am grateful for James Jordan's suggestions regarding the original angelic training of man. He suggests that this was Satan's original mission and purpose: to teach and train Adam and Eve, but he rebelled and tempted the woman into sin.

there is still something of an eschatological glory suggested, something which the human race points toward and longs to attain. In that moment in the fiery furnace, the indestructibility of the three faithful young men prefigures something of the glorified state of humanity, pointing forward toward something like the transfiguration of Jesus. Hebrews celebrates this expectation in the glorification of Jesus above the angels (Heb. 1). Jesus is the faithful Son who has been exalted and crowned with glory and honor so that he might bring many sons to that glory (Heb. 2:10). The glorified state of humanity is to a position higher than the angels, but prior to that, angels stood in our place.

## THE SONS OF GOD IN JOB

This has been a long detour on the "sons of God," but it is entirely necessary and hopefully helpful for understanding the rest of the book of Job. From this vantage, we can suggest that the "sons of God" who present themselves before Yahweh are those men and angels who would have access to the presence of God. These might be angelic beings, perhaps even entirely so, but these may also be prophets who, as we suggested in the first chapter, have been granted access to the counsels of Yahweh. Some of these sons of God stood up and shouted for joy in the heavenly council when the cornerstone of the earth was laid (Job 39:6–7). There is another glimpse into a heavenly assembly with both men and angels in 1 Kings 22:19–23 where Micaiah relates the deliberations of the heavenly court regarding Yahweh's design to "persuade Ahab to go up, that he may fall at Ramoth Gilead." While the title "sons of God" is not explicitly used, the scene matches the descriptions suggested thus far, and establishes the fact that sometimes people may be present (e.g., Micaiah the prophet). Regardless of who was actually there in the court in Job 1:6, biblically, this title can be applied to both angels and men, those who have access to the presence of God, those who bear the image and have the authorization to represent the Father to the world, carrying on his mission in the world. Those are the sons of God.

This is what we see in Job 1:6. The sons of God present themselves before Yahweh. The word "to present themselves" is a word that can indicate an official presence in court (Num. 11:16; Deut. 31:14; Josh. 24:1; Ps. 2:2). The sons of God are his servants, his chief advisers, those who stand at the ready in his presence. Imagine the court of a great King who is seated in all his glory, and all of his subjects come before him, but he has particular princes and nobles who *stand* in his presence. The nobles, princes, advisers, and counselors stand around him in his presence. The sons of God are those nobility, princes, and royalty that station themselves in the presence of God.

The idea of "presenting themselves" also suggests images of worship and covenant renewal. The same word is used when Israel was led out of Egypt by the mighty arm of Yahweh, and they "took their stand at the foot of the mountain" (Ex. 19:17). The seventy elders of Israel, likewise, are to be brought to the tent of meeting and take their stand with Moses (Num. 11:16). At the end of Joshua's life, he called all the tribes of Israel with their elders and judges and officers, and they "presented themselves before God" for a review and renewal of the covenant (Josh. 24:1). The word is also used of God's own presence in coming to speak to his people. The Lord stands and presents himself before Moses on Mount Sinai (Ex. 34:5), and likewise he stands before Samuel and calls to the young man (1 Sam. 3:10). This heavenly assembly is like a worship service. Like the Apostle John's Revelation, readers are granted entry into heaven. The veil separating earth and heaven is drawn back, and we see the heavenly assembly gathered around the throne of God, an assembly of angels and men gathered in obedience, allegiance, and worship.

In Revelation, one of the things that the angels and living creatures are doing is "blessing" the Lord God who reigns forever and ever (Rev. 5:12–13). In this heavenly scene in Job 1, the discussion has everything to do with whether Job will "bless" God or "curse" him. As the narrative unfolds, Job joins the worship of heaven proleptically in response to the first set of calamities, and this action prefigures and previews an even greater fulfillment coming in the resolution of the epilogue. After he has received the news of the four disasters that have struck his house, Job tears his robe and falls to the ground and worships God, blessing him as the one who gives and takes away (1:21).

## The Satan

The text says that "Satan also came in among them." The name "Satan" means "accuser" or "adversary." What is particularly striking is that here, and throughout the book of Job, his name is spelled with a definite article. His name is "The Satan," not just "Satan." The definite article aims to underline his role. He is the accuser, the adversary. What's he doing? He's *the* accuser who has come *to accuse*. He's the accuser of the brethren (Rev. 12:10), and as the adversary, he is the prosecuting attorney. His name is what he does. This is explicit in Zechariah 3:1 where Zechariah witnesses a similar heavenly court-like setting, and "The Satan" is seen standing at the right hand of Yahweh to "accuse" Joshua, the high priest. The verb is formed with the same consonants as the subject noun: *satan*. Zechariah 3 is one of the only other places where the definite article shows up attached to Satan's name. There, as in Job 1, the role of the definite article clearly functions to underline this role as accuser or adversary. Many commentators insist that the article indicates that this character is a generic "accuser/adversary" and therefore not the same person as the Devil, Satan. While this is perhaps technically possible, there is no other evidence for this hypothesis, and plenty of corroborating evidence which makes the traditional reading natural. For example, Satan plays a similar role in 1 Chronicles 21:1 where he incites David to take a sinful census of Israel. While the word certainly can show up in more generic contexts, as in Psalm 109, picturing human enemies as accusers, adversaries, and prosecuting attorneys (Ps. 109:4, 6, 20, 29), Peter seems to have Job 1 in mind when he describes the devil as an "adversary" who prowls "around like a roaring lion seeking someone to devour" (1 Pet. 5:8). This is reminiscent of the Satan's answer to Yahweh regarding his "going to and fro on the earth" and "walking back and forth on it" (Job 1:7).

One question that may occur to some readers is, "What exactly is Satan doing in heaven?" There are several answers to this, but from a purely literary angle, Satan clearly *belongs* here. If this is another Adam story, if we're in the garden, or somewhere near the garden (symbolically), and there are lots of animals, a perfect man ruling, *of course* Satan is going to show up. That's what happened in Genesis 3. All the same characters are in play. Looking ahead to the end of chapter 2, Job's wife is also going to show up, encouraging Job to do what the Satan wants, "tempting" her husband with the very words of Satan (2:9). The prologue of Job opens with an Adam, an Eve, the Satan, and God. All the characters are present and accounted for.

Even with the literary parallels, it may still seem somewhat curious for Satan to show up in the *heavenly* courtroom. In Genesis 3, Satan was in the Garden of Eden. How did Satan get into heaven? Who let him in? While the text does not say explicitly, there are several clues scattered throughout the pages of Scripture. First, consider Genesis 3 again. Even here no explanation is given for why Satan is in the Garden of Eden with Adam and Eve. It may not be heaven proper, but the Garden of Eden was heaven on earth, a place where God and man walked and talked together in perfect harmony. How did Satan get in *there*? Suggestions have been made that Adam should have guarded the garden more faithfully and protected his wife, but at the same time, in a perfect, sinless world, it is difficult to imagine what a "threat" might look like or feel like.[2] Secondly, and more to the point, Revelation 12 recounts the story of the incarnation beginning with the birth of the male child who was to rule all nations with a rod of iron (Rev. 12:5). A dragon is said to be seeking the child to devour him, but he is caught up by God. Here war breaks out in heaven with Michael and his angels fighting with the dragon and his angels (Rev. 12:7). Ultimately the dragon and his angels "did not prevail nor was a place found for

---

2. James Jordan suggests that the devil had not actually "fallen" until he tempted Eve to sin. That was his rebellion. Thus initially, his presence in the garden may have been as legitimate as any other angel.

them in heaven any longer" (Rev. 12:8). The text goes on to say that the dragon was cast out, and John identifies the dragon as "that serpent of old, called the Devil and Satan" (Rev. 12:9). Piecing this together, Satan must have had some sort of place or standing in heaven prior to the ascension of Jesus. Jesus seems to be referring to the end of this arrangement when speaking of his coming crucifixion and says, "Now is the judgment of this world: now will the ruler of this world be cast out" (John 12:31).

It appears that in the Old Covenant, Satan still had significant authority and played some part in the heavenly assemblies. Again, consider 2 Chronicles 18, the parallel to the episode already noted in 1 Kings 22, where the prophet Micaiah was present and witnessed the Lord authorizing a "lying spirit" to fill the mouths of the prophets in order to deceive Ahab and lead him into disaster (2 Chron. 18:18–22). This heavenly courtroom once again contains at least one shady angelic creature. Who is this "lying spirit" anyway? The implication seems to be that there might be any number of angelic beings (good and bad) present in the divine court. One of the great glories of the New Covenant, then, is the significant change that has occurred *in heaven*. In place of the accuser we have Jesus, our advocate with the Father; our high priest who intercedes for us. In place of lying spirits, we have fellow Christians and the martyrs around the throne worshiping God and crying out "how long?" (Rev. 6:9–10). In fact, Paul says that all Christians have been raised with Christ and seated in the heavenly places (Eph. 2).

This scene is also surprising for Yahweh's response to the Satan in his court. God seems far too friendly to the Satan. He almost seems eager to oblige the accuser, eager to provide the Satan with someone to prosecute. God points Job out, "have you considered my servant Job, there is none like him on the earth," and he repeats what the narrator has already told us, "a blameless and upright man, one who fears God and shuns evil" (1:8; cf. 1:1). It's as though Yahweh can hardly contain himself with enthusiasm for Job. He has the excitement of a father who wants to tell everyone about the latest and greatest achievements of his son. The Satan, however, is not impressed, and immediately sets in accusing him. "Does Job fear God for nothing?" (1:9). Haven't you protected him on every side? (1:10) He's weak. If you just move your hand out of the way, he'll curse you to your face, I promise (1:11). The Satan arrives on the scene and immediately begins accusing. He's not only accusing Job of weakness, he is also accusing God of propping up this weakness, subsidizing Job's hypocrisy. Satan accuses Job of only obeying God out of fear of punishment or loss of blessing, and accuses God of protecting this shallow obedience. The issue at stake is the nature of God's relationship with Job. Is their relationship built on genuine love, or does Job only fear God on a contractual basis? In other words, Yahweh celebrates Job as a son in whom he delights, but the Satan suggests that their relationship is a sterile *quid pro quo* agreement. Job, the Satan implies, does not love God as his father. If Yahweh removes his hedge of protection, Job will no longer fear God and will "curse" him to his face.

Notice God's designation of Job as his "servant" (1:8). On the one hand this designation seems to be full of love and admiration, but on the other hand it's almost disturbing given the context. It's all well and good for a father to brag on his son, but is it really a good idea for a father to brag on his son to a thug, an assassin and sworn enemy? Satan is on the prowl for a victim and God offers him one. "Have you considered *my servant* Job?" We noted in the preface that Job is one of those books that many Christians try to avoid for this reason. Not only is it long and kind of complicated, but we are also afraid of the God in the book of Job. We are afraid of a God who might treat us like *that*. It is easy to read this and hope that God doesn't call us his "servants." There is also the question of evil in the world and God's part in it. Isn't God our defender, our protector? Does God *have* to give Satan something to do, someone to devour? Why doesn't he just throw a ball and distract him? Must Yahweh offer Satan a victim?

However, God's words keep coming back to Job. "Have you considered my servant Job, how blameless and how perfect he is?" God is bragging on his servant Job and egging Satan on. "Strike him. I dare you." Does God routinely do that to his people?

Not only is Yahweh a God who gives permission to the Satan to strike Job, Satan knows that God must stretch out his hand (1:11). The Lord says to Satan, "behold all that he has is in your power, only do not lay a hand on his person" (1:12). Satan knows that the hand of God holds even *his* hand. The hand of God holds the hand of Satan. Satan's hand cannot move apart from the hand of God. This is the historic orthodox doctrine of providence summarized in the Westminster Confession of Faith in the following words: "God, the great Creator of all things, doth uphold, direct dispose, and govern all creatures, actions, and things, from the greatest even to the least, by his most wise and holy providence, according to his infallible foreknowledge, and the free and immutable counsel of his own will, to the praise of the glory of his wisdom, power, justice, goodness, and mercy" (WCF, V.1).

### CONCLUSION: SONS PRESENT AND ABSENT

What does this first section of Job teach us? One of the stronger motifs running through these first verses is the theme of sons. Job has seven sons. His sons feast. Job is the greatest of the sons of the East; he is a son, he has sons, and he offers sacrifices for his sons. The sons of God appear before the Lord. Based on this early repetition, it is safe to assume that one of the major themes of Job is about what it means to be a son of God.

The great problem raised by this first section is the disconnect between heaven and earth, between Job and God. The great horror is the fact that a righteous, blameless "son" does not stand before the presence of God his Father. Job is the "greatest of the sons of the east," but he is not among the "sons of God" who present themselves in the divine assembly. Why is Job not there? Is it just for Job not to be there? This connects to the familial theme as well.

What does it mean to be God's son? What does it mean to be loved like a son? What is the nature of that relationship? One of the early clues to the answers of these questions is in the parallel between fathers in the text. Job is a father and God is a father. Both have sons. The narrator shows us two faithful fathers, and what

God is doing to Job here is exactly what Job is doing for his sons. Job, as a faithful father, offers up sacrifices for his sons. He says, "This is my firstborn," and cuts him up, puts him on the altar, and watches him go up to God in smoke. Then he takes his second born and cuts him, puts him on the altar, and sends him up into the presence of God. Now God is doing it to Job.

God says, "This is my son, Job, have you considered him?" God's love for Job draws Job into his presence. He wants Job to pass back through the cherubim into his presence. When God loves his people, he wants them with him. Notice the parallel here with Jesus. As soon as God says, "this is my beloved Son, in whom I am well pleased" at Jesus' baptism, what happens? The Spirit drives him into the wilderness to be tempted by the devil (Matt. 3:17–4:1; Mark 1:11–12; Luke 3:22; 4:1). God drives his beloved Son into battle. After that initial victory, the same Spirit drives Jesus into Galilee to do battle with demons and hypocrites and all manner of uncleanness. The Spirit does not push Jesus forward aimlessly; the Spirit presses Jesus forward on the mission of God to draw his Son back up into his presence. The Spirit ultimately drives Jesus to the cross, into the grave, out of the tomb, and on the other side of that great struggle, he is drawn back up into the presence of the Father.

When God gets excited about his sons, he wants to send them into battle. He sends his sons into the fray. "This is my son!" he announces proudly, and then he sends him to face Satan. "This is my son!" and he sends him to battle demons. "This is my son!" He sends him to face false accusations, to be mocked, spat upon, and beaten to a bloody pulp. When God loves his sons, he sends them into battle. If God did not spare his own Son in his love, how much more so will he love all of his beloved sons? His love is not aimless; it is not sadistic. His love rejoices in the glory that comes after the battle, the glory of victory, and preeminently the glory of communion with him.

This kind of love only makes sense if the resurrection is true. If the resurrection is true, then God knows what's on the other side of the sword. He knows what's on the other side of the fire—life with him. On the other side of the battle, there is no doubt of being raised up into wholeness and fullness in his presence. For whom the Lord loves, he chastens and scourges every son whom he receives (Heb. 12:6). He takes his sons, pours his Spirit upon them, and draws them to himself through the sword and fire. That is what Job is doing with his sons, and that is what God is doing with his servant, his beloved son, Job.

# 4

## FROM GOOD TO VERY GOOD: JOB 1:13–22

In the beginning, God created the heavens and the earth. The Bible begins in Genesis with the story of creation, where we are first introduced to God and, specifically, the Spirit of God. In the beginning, when and where God created the heavens and the earth, Moses tells us that the earth was without form and void, darkness was on the face of the deep, and the Spirit of God was hovering over the face of the waters (Gen. 1:2). When we are first introduced to God, in person, in action, we're introduced to God the Spirit. The word for Spirit is *ruach*, which means "wind" or "breath." The *ruach* of God is the wind or breath of God hovering over the face of the waters.

This is the set-up for the rest of Genesis 1, which is concerned with the construction of the universe. The chief builder, the one in charge of the building project, is the Spirit of God. The Spirit—the

Wind of God—is the one enacting this work. The Spirit of God hovering over the face of the waters does not merely mean that the Spirit of God is going to watch the show; the Spirit is not just there as a spectator. Rather, he is the one coming to *do it*. When God spoke, and when we speak, breath comes out. Speaking means pushing air across vocal chords, vibrating them, and flinging that sound out into the world. Likewise it is the wind of God, the breath of God, which rushes out as the first words are spoken in the history of the world. When God says let there be light, and there was light, the Spirit of God is at work: it's the Spirit of God enacting the Word of the Father in creation (cf. Col. 1:15–16; Heb. 1:1–3).

We should also ask how this wind of God creates the world. How does the Spirit of God build the universe? In addition to speaking/blowing creation into being, God created and constructed his world through introducing *divisions*. After he created light, he divided the light from the darkness. He broke them apart and called the light "day," and the darkness he called "night." On the second day when he created the firmament, he spread it out in the midst of the waters above and below, and he *divided* the waters. On the third day, God said, let the waters under the heavens be gathered into one place and let dry ground appear. Again, the Spirit's construction work consists of dividing. While the waters were gathered together into one place, there was still simultaneously an implicit division being made between the waters and all the dry ground. On the fourth day, God put the lights into the firmament of the heavens to divide the day from the night and for signs and seasons, and days and years. God spoke, the wind blew and the sun and the moon and the stars exploded in the heavens to divide between night and day, seasons and years.

The great and last division in the creation week occured on the sixth day when God created the first man. God's hurricane word pushed dirt up together and created the man, breathing life into him, and then he said it's not good that he should be alone. He put the man into a deep sleep, and took a rib out of his side. We've read the passage so many times we miss the violence of the act. Of course it is not malicious violence, but we should not ignore the cutting, tearing, popping, and breaking that would have occurred in that first surgery. God tore a rib out of Adam, and God the Spirit has divided again. He tore a rib out of Adam and with that rib created the woman. The Spirit of God is this breath, this wind, this storm of God enacting the work of creation through the word of God. One of the hallmarks of this wind-Spirit is his dividing things and breaking them apart. Like the woman Adam meets as he wakes up, the Spirit divides not just for the sake of dividing. His aim is glory and beauty, and to put the pieces back together in new and beautiful ways.

One more note here before returning to the text of Job: recall the way that God evaluates his work. After he has created something, his typical judgment is that it is "good." He created light, and he saw that it was good (Gen. 1:4). Likewise, he gathered the seas into one place and the dry ground appeared, and God saw that it was good (Gen. 1:10). Running through Genesis 1, we find God creating these things and calling them good (Gen. 1:12, 18, 21, 25). As others have pointed out, the first time something is "not good" is somewhat startling. This negative evaluation comes when God sees that Adam is alone. So we have good, good, good, good, good, good, and not good, even though it ends with a "very good" (Gen. 1:31).

The point can be seen from two angles, two sides of the same coin. First, the action of saying that something is good doesn't imply that it's done or finished. We might ask: if something is good, why does God come back the next day? The implicit answer of Genesis is because there's more to be done. Just because something is "good" doesn't mean that it's completed. The declaration that something is good is not that it is *finished*, but that it is good *for now*, good for today, and it is *ready* for later, ready for tomorrow. Second, we should not miss the fact that there can be "not good" in a perfect world. In a sinless, perfect world it was "not good" for Adam to be alone. Presumably, Adam in himself was a "good" creation, but that bachelor status was superseded in time by the need for something or in this case *someone* that would improve Adam and make him better. Time is a gift of God, part of his good creation. Thus God's evaluation of his own work depends upon time. *When* are we? Creation can be "good" for now, and good means that it is ready for what is coming next. The Spirit of God creates things, the Word says they are good, and then God can come back the next day and *because* they are good, he is ready to divide them and do something new with them. Apart from growing into this newness the good is "not good."

This is a hard lesson to learn in life. We collapse time into an eternal present and evaluate our lives, children, marriages, jobs—everything—on the standard of *eternity*; but even God doesn't do that. God created light, separated it from darkness, named the light Day and the darkness Night, saw that it was good and then got a good night's rest. Talk about small beginnings, but God himself was very pleased with his first day's work, and his people need to learn this wisdom. This means learning to ask *when* we are. Sin is the great complicater, and frequently past failures make evaluating progress more complex and messy. Christians are new creations in Christ, and while this does not mean that every consequence of sin magically disappears, it does mean a genuinely new start, a new beginning, a new genesis. This is what the Bible calls grace. Christians must believe God, trust the work of the Spirit, and cling to Jesus. This means learning to work hard each day and then to sit back with thankful hearts knowing that if there is any fruit or harvest, it will have been only by the kindness and blessing of God. More practically it means evaluating where we are, when we are, and working for more glory in faith. A family with young children will have a certain goodness and glory, while a couple with grown children and grandchildren will have another sort of goodness and glory. In God's mercy, it is a *growing* goodness and glory. Our "goods" are being turned into "very goods," and this means obedience, faith, and patience.

On the flip side, it should be noted that there are many opportunities for sinners to resent this God-given pattern. How many disasters have occurred because children were not raised to *leave* the home? How often are people tempted to cling to the first good and try to prevent the division that must necessarily come in order to inherit the "very good"? This comes in many forms: a spouse, children, children with special needs, health problems, loss of a job, financial hardships, a new boss, or a new teacher. God, and God the Spirit in particular, loves to press forward, to take the "good" and transform it into the glory of "very good." This means walking by faith on paths that are sometimes very difficult, and fighting many temptations to bitterness and resentment toward the wisdom of the Sprit of God and those whom he uses to call us toward glory.

## THE WIND AND JOB

Job is the greatest of the sons of the east (1:3), but one of the great problems in the first twelve verses is that he is not among the sons of God. The sons of God are those men and angels that gather before the throne of God, who have access to the royal counsels of God. In the place of Job we have the Accuser, the Satan, the Adversary among the sons of God (1:6). This "problem" is at the same time a great hint at what God is doing. The Lord is beginning to raise Job up as his son. Job offers sacrifices for his sons according to their number, in effect saying, "God, have you considered my son?" and offers him up to God. In the following scene in heaven, we see something very similar going on in God's own words. Satan comes in among the sons of God, and the Lord says, "Have you considered my servant Job?" God offers Job up, continuing the work of raising him up as his son. As Job loves and cares for his sons, so Yahweh loves Job, his son.

We began our consideration of Job by underlining the fact that Job is an Adam in a garden-like setting in the east, like the Garden of Eden. He has been fruitful and has multiplied: he is surrounded with animals that he rules over, and his children are always feasting, but even perfect Adam was not finished. He was not yet glorified. The hint of coming glory is in the creation of Eve. If Job is an Adam, we should see Job as an Adam in the calamities that fall upon him. Job is not only an Adam in perfection and harmony and goodness, he is also an Adam as he is struck by the hand of God, cut open, and broken in order to be glorified. God is taking blameless Job—his Adam—and offering him to Satan, much like he did to the first Adam in the garden. God allowed *that* serpent into the garden. God offers this beloved son and says, have you considered my servant Job? Yahweh of course knows what he is doing. He offers his son to be cut in order to be glorified. Just as Adam was cut, just as his rib was torn out, he offers Job so that he can create him again with more glory. In this way, we ought to understand Job as being "blameless" and "upright" as parallel to the evaluation of creation as "good." Job, as he is introduced to us, is in the midst of creation. God sees Job and says that he is "good," but we know how the Spirit loves to blow and divide and renew his "good" creation so that it can become "very good."

### THE CALAMITIES

Verse 13 begins with "there was a day when his sons and daughters were eating and drinking wine in their oldest brother's house." It's on *that* day, and the text comes back to that, when the last messenger comes to tell him about his sons and daughters: "While he was still speaking, another also came and said your sons and daughters were eating and drinking wine in their oldest brother's house" (1:18). So the first set of calamities is framed by the sons and daughters feasting. Norman Habel has pointed out that 1:13 also begins with the same time stamp as 1:6, "Now there was a day." The day that the sons of God assembled before Yahweh corresponded to the day that Job's sons and daughters were feasting in the oldest brother's house.[1]

The framing of the calamities creates a feeling of simultaneity. The sons and daughters are feasting, and meanwhile these calamities are falling on Job's house. The literary structure reminds me of the end of *The Godfather*. Michael Corleone is at his nephew's church service, and as Michael is taking his vows to become Godfather, the movie is fading in and out of that scene, flashing to individuals who pose a threat to the family being shot and strangled.

---

1. Norman C. Habel, *The Book of Job: A Commentary* (Philadelphia: Westminster Press, 1985), 91.

The threats are eliminated one by one. If we were to do the movie version of Job, while the children are feasting in their oldest brother's house, calamities are striking the house of Job. Fire is falling from heaven, the Sabians are coming and raiding and killing. Then the Chaldeans come with three bands, and the camera is zooming in and out, flashing from feasting to calamity over and over. Finally, the last messenger comes. "While he was still speaking . . . your sons and daughters were eating and drinking in their oldest brother's house, and a great wind came across the wilderness and struck the four corners of the house and it fell on the young people and they are dead and I alone have escaped to tell you."

There's also a clear literary structure and chiastic order to the calamities. The children feasting are the bookends (1:13, 18–19), but the first and the third disasters are also parallel: the Sabians are a foreign enemy who strike Job's herds of oxen and donkeys. The animals are stolen, and the servants are killed by the edge of the sword (1:15). Then in verse 17, in the third disaster, another messenger appears reporting that the Chaldeans, another foreign enemy, formed three bands, raided the camels, took them away, and killed the servants with the edge of the sword. At the center is verse 16, the second disaster that falls. "And while he was still speaking, another came and said 'the fire of God fell from heaven and burned up the sheep and the servants and consumed them and I alone have escaped to tell you.' " This calamity is different. No foreigners are involved in this one. The fire from heaven burns the animals and everything is consumed. As is frequently the case with this kind of literary structure, the center is the key to understanding what is taking place.

A. Sons and daughters eating and drinking (1:13)
> B. Oxen and donkeys stolen and servants killed by the edge of the sword (1:14–15)
>> C. Fire of God fell and burned up the sheep and servants and consumed them (1:16)
> B' Camels stolen and servants killed by the edge of the sword (1:17)

A' Sons and daughters eating and drinking
> C' A great wind struck the house and they are dead (1:18–19)

The "fire of God" falls from heaven and consumes the sheep and the servants. God's presence on Mount Sinai (Deut. 4:11; 9:15) and the fire that fills the tabernacle at its dedication is a similar fire (Ex. 40:34–38; cf. 1 Kings 8:10–11). This is part of the fire that continually burns on the altar before the Lord (Lev. 6:12). In other words, the language describing the calamites in Job 1:13–19 is sacrificial. Think of Elijah on Mount Carmel with the prophets of Baal (1 Kings 18:20–40). The contest is all about whose God is going to send down fire and consume the offering. It's Yahweh, the God of Israel, who comes with his fire and consumes both the offering and the altar that Elijah had prepared. When we look at the calamities that befall Job in light of this sacrificial imagery, a number of other parallels emerge.[2]

We have already suggested that there was a parallel between Job offering up sacrifices for his sons according to the number of his sons and daughters, and God "offering" Job. Job, as father, offers up his sons through sacrifices. Yahweh, also as a father, offers up Job like a son to the sacrificial fire of these calamities. The fire is clear, it falls as the fire of God from heaven, and as in the Ascension Offering, everything is consumed by fire and goes up in smoke. Throughout Leviticus, frequently the offerings of God are referred to as the bread of God, the food of God (e.g., Lev. 21:6, 8, 17, 21–22). God consumes the

---

2. Here and what follows on the sacrificial symbolism is taken substantially from my essay "Father Storm" in *The Glory of Kings: A Festschrift for James B. Jordan* (Eugene, OR:Wipf and Stock, 2011).

offerings on the altar and they rise to him, and he is satisfied. In Job 1:16, the fire of God "eats" the sheep and servants, and only one servant escapes alive to tell Job. This ties the bookend feasting of the children into the center of the scene. Many of the sacrifices include portions that would be eaten by the priests (e.g., Lev. 6:25–26) or the worshipper (e.g., Lev. 7:11–18). Consequently, a sacrifice was frequently also a feast.

Remember that the Ascension Offering required that the animal be cut up into pieces and put on the altar where it was consumed by the fire and ascended as smoke to the presence of God. In 1:15 and 1:17, the killing of the servants by the edge of the sword is highlighted. The edge of the sword is central to preparing a sacrifice.

The final calamity is also parallel to the center of this section in that it is another natural disaster: the wind that knocks the four corners of the house down. It's not people—not Chaldeans or Sabians—but a great wind. Here there are at least two indications that a sacrificial motif is in view. First, the great wind is a great *ruach*, the word for the Spirit-wind which can refer to a natural occurrence of wind, but is also frequently associated with the storm presence of the Spirit of God who comes to create (Gen. 1:1; 8:1; Ps. 33:6) and judge (Ex. 14:21; 15:8–10; Ps. 18:7–15; 35:5). When Yahweh draws near to his people, he frequently comes as a great storm (Ex. 19:16; 20:18), and it is this same fire-storm presence of the Spirit that leads Israel through the wilderness and fills the tabernacle (Ex. 40:34–38). With the "fire of God" at the center of the calamities, this great wind should also be seen as part of the hand of God (1:11).[3]

The second indication that this great wind should be viewed in sacrificial terms is the reference to the "four corners" of the house that are struck (1:19). The most common use of this description of "four corners" is in the descriptions of the tabernacle in Exodus and the temple in Ezekiel's vision. In Exodus, it is only the bronze altar that has the same four "corners" as the house that Job's children are

---

3. Both the fire and the wind remind us of the life of Elijah who witnessed the fire of God falling to consume his offering on Mount Carmel and who was also later taken up in the whirlwind and fire of God.

killed in (Ex. 27:2; 38:2).[4] In Ezekiel's vision, the four corners almost exclusively refer to the four corners of the altar and the four corners of the temple court (Ezek. 43:16; 43:20; 45:19; 46:21; 46:22). Specifically, the same word appears to describe the four corners of Ezekiel's altar where blood is to be smeared (Ezek. 43:20; 45:19). Job's entire household is an altar, and now Job's world has been consumed by the fire of God from heaven, and the blood of his children and servants is smeared on the four corners of his house.

This sacrificial imagery makes the parallels between Job as father and God as Father explicit. There are two fathers in the prologue of Job, and there are at least two sets of sons. The first father is Job who is perfect and upright, who fears God and shuns evil, and he sanctifies his sons by offering up Ascension Offerings according to their number. Yahweh is also a faithful and perfect Father, and he is likewise concerned with sanctifying his son Job and does so by offering him up in the sacrificial swords and fire of disaster. In both cases there are substitutes. Job's sons are offered up through the mediation of animals, while Job is offered up through the mediation of his entire household. As an Ascension Offering is cut apart, arranged on the altar, and entirely consumed in the fire, so Job's household is dismembered and consumed in the fire-wind of God.

There will be more to say later, but the fact that these calamities come one after another through the words of messengers and servants is significant. Job does not witness the calamities; rather, they come in the first instance in the form of words. When God creates, he speaks and the Spirit blows the Word of God into being. The creation pattern holds even when he de-creates and in Job's calamities we see this. The Spirit-storm of God's presence has fallen and systematically broken apart Job's world, but it comes in four "days" of reports. There are four messengers, four reports, four words announcing what has taken place. The Spirit blows the Word into being, and here we see Job's world torn apart. This

---

4. The altar also has four "ends" in Exodus 27:4 and again in Exodus 38:5. Different words are used to describe the four corners of the ark (Ex. 25:12; 37:3) and the four corners of the table of showbread (Ex. 25:26; 37:13). Literally, the ark has four "feet," while the table of showbread has four "corner-sides."

Adam, this beloved son, is being divided in order to be remade, torn in order to be healed, and broken in order to be glorified.

### A BLAMELESS SACRIFICE

If it is not yet clear that this sacrificial imagery is purposeful, there is another angle from which to view the same thing. Arguably, the prologue of Job goes out of its way to emphasize and identify Job as a *sacrificial* victim. Just as sacrificial animals must be *tamim*, that is, perfect, without blemish (Lev. 1:3), Job is described as *tam*, perfect, blameless. So that this is not missed, it is repeated three times, once by the narrator (1:1) and twice by Yahweh himself (1:8; 2:3). Job also insists that this is true of himself, though he is criticized by his friends for it (4:6; 9:20–21). Lest we be distracted by the fact that it is Job's servants, animals, and children that are consumed, they too are described in terms of perfection, adding up to tens: seven sons and three daughters, seven thousand sheep and three thousand camels, and five hundred oxen and five hundred female donkeys (1:2–3). Job is without blemish, and his household is presented in similar fashion.

We have heard this description of perfection before: Abraham is referred to as the servant of Yahweh and called to be blameless (Gen. 17:1). Noah and Jacob were also blameless before God (Gen. 6:9; 25:27). This status and calling did not mean that any of them were exempt from trials and suffering. In fact, each of these men faced significant trials, struggles, and suffering, and it is the sacrificial connotations of being "blameless" that offer some helpful commentary. The description "without blemish" is used nearly thirty times in Leviticus and Numbers and always to describe the kind of animal that is eligible for sacrifice. This is because God is holy and without blemish (Deut. 32:4). God is attracted to the blameless; perfection is what catches his eye. God teaches Israel to imitate him. *Have you considered that ram of mine? Not a blemish; he'd make a great sacrifice.* Of course the echo there is intentional. God takes notice of his blameless people; he is attracted to them and points them out. "Have you considered my servant Job, that there is none like him on the earth, a blameless and upright man?" (1:8). God is blameless and perfect, loving the blameless and perfect and seeking to draw them to himself. His presence is a hurricane of glory. God is a fierce storm, and when he draws near, mountains quake, the earth cracks, seas rage, and men tremble and fear. The storm of God's presence creates, judges, separates, and re-creates. The wind of God divides and tears apart before reuniting and healing. The very good God loves to take good men, break them apart, and turn them into very good men. The perfect and glorious God loves to take perfect men, break them apart, and turn them into greater glory and greater perfection.

## JOB'S FIRST RESPONSE

Job responds to these first disasters by tearing his clothing, shaving his head, and falling to the ground. All of this is reenactment of the following verse: "Naked I came from my mother's womb, and naked I shall return there" (1:21). Notice even more Adam-like imagery. Job is naked and returning to the ground, to the dust of which he was made. He says he wants to return to his mother's womb, which seems strange. Does Job really mean that? Do humans really return to their mothers' wombs? He may only be referring to the ground; the ground was the first "mother" of Adam. Out of the ground Adam was created, and Job wants to return there. In other words, Job wants to die, but the fact that he's saying that he is going to return to a womb also suggests some latent hope. Returning to a womb, even in death, suggests a faint glimmer of hope in a new life ahead. Wombs are ordinarily places of new life. His statement conjures an image which reminds us of Nicodemus's question many centuries later (John 3:1–8). Can a grown man return and go back into his mother's womb? Jesus says that he *must*, and Job says that he will.

The Spirit is still at work in Job. In all of this, Job is still blameless and upright; he did not sin (1:22). Job is a blameless Adam. What did he do to deserve these hardships? In one sense, we might say nothing, but in another sense, we have shown that Job is everything that God loves. Job is a beloved son, and God is glorifying his beloved son. God is growing him up and is taking him from glory to glory. As we noted in the creation narrative, even in perfection and goodness, there is always a pressing forward. "Good" always anticipates "very good." Good does not mean finished, good means good for today and ready for tomorrow. Between the "good" and the "very good" there is division, separation, and surgery. Ribs are pulled apart, animals are cut up and placed on the altar. It is only when the beloved son is worked over with the fire-Wind of God that he begins to participate in that "very good," in the life of the Father, the Word, and the Wind. As G.K. Chesterton put it, "in the prologue we see Job tormented not because he was the worst of men, but because he was the best."[5] In other words, Job's goodness and integrity are not arguments against Job's suffering; they are the very reasons *for* it.

### JUSTIFICATION AND TRIBULATION

We can also make the same point approaching this from a more formal theological angle. The term "justification" means to declare one righteous, to reckon a sinner righteous for the sake of Jesus the Righteous One. In historic Protestant orthodoxy, the doctrine of justification has been viewed as central, and the great Reformers and Reformation confessions insisted that this justified status was received by faith alone, for the sake of Christ's death and resurrection, simultaneously pardoning the sin of humans for the sake of the stricken Savior on the cross while imputing the righteousness of Jesus to the sinner in history.[6] In other words, the blameless, sacrificial quality of Jesus—that which qualified him to be the Lamb of God who takes away the sins of the world—that status has been imputed to those who cling to him in faith.

Paul seems to recognize this in Romans 5 where he famously summarizes that since we have been justified by faith and have peace with God and access to his grace, *we also glory in tribulations*

---

5. G.K. Chesterton, *Introduction to The Book of Job*, http://www.chesterton.org/wordpress/2011/07/introduction-to-the-book-of-job/

6. See Westminster Shorter Catechism Question 33.

(Rom. 5:1–3). No sooner has Paul declared our justified status in Christ then he turns to trials and suffering. He seems to think that they belong *together*. Paul says justification and immediately thinks of suffering: "and not only *that* [justification], but we also glory in tribulations" (Rom. 5:3). Justification continues as the theme running through the following chapters as Paul addresses why there is remaining sin in the believer and what this means for Israel, but his argument climaxes in chapter 12 where he writes, "I beseech you therefore, brethren by the mercies of God, that you present your bodies a living sacrifice, holy, acceptable to God which is your reasonable service" (Rom. 12:1). In other words, for Paul, the point of justification is sacrifice. The point of being declared "without blemish" is that we are now qualified to be dismembered and arranged on the altar. The imputation of the righteousness of Christ means that we may now be lit on fire, and of course, that is precisely what God does. He sends his Spirit upon his justified people, and every time he does so, a Pentecost breaks out. Every time he declares a person righteous, God lights them on fire and the Spirit begins his sacrificial work, consuming our dross, and turning us into Spirit-smoke, drawing us up into the whirlwind.[7]

This means that Hebrews 12 is frequently misread. After describing the new Mount Zion, the city of the Living God, the general assembly and church of the firstborn, the spirits of just men made perfect, and Jesus the mediator of the new covenant, the warning is to not turn away (Heb. 12:22–25). We may not leave the mountain, but we must worship at this mountain in reverence and fear and hear the Word as it thunders (Heb. 12:26–28). The very last verse declares "for our God is a consuming fire." Too frequently that final statement is read as a warning, but the warning has already been stated. The warning is that we may not leave or ignore the voice that shakes the earth and heaven. We may not trifle with the things of God like Nadab and Abihu.

---

7. Many of the ideas in this previous paragraph and some of what follows were originally published in an article in *Credenda Agenda* entitled "Prequalified Sacrifices."

God's consuming fire is not just a warning. The fact that God consumes with fire is a *promise*. God is a consuming fire, and he's at work consuming *us*. This is what Pentecost means. The fire of God comes down from heaven to set his people on fire, to light the living sacrifices. The Wind of God comes rushing through the upper room and sets his blameless servants ablaze. That is what God is doing at Pentecost. That is what God is doing with Job, and that is what God always does with his justified people. The Spirit comes, the Spirit is poured out to create and recreate, but the Spirit also burns, divides, destroys, and breaks down in order to make new. The proof of the Spirit's presence is in us. Every human experiences some of this, but believers know that they have been broken. Christians know what it is like for the Spirit to be at work in their lives. Christians have cuts and scars and bruises.

Unfortunately, Christians frequently see their cuts and scars and bruises and fall into despair and hopelessness. Part of the lesson of Job is that this is completely reversed. The scars, the brokenness, the fact that it hurts, means that the Spirit is at work. The only question is: how will we respond to the work of the Spirit? Will we try to give him the strong-arm and try to get away? Others simply grow tired and close up, rejecting the good work of the Spirit, grieving the Spirit that sealed us, but the scars are for *glory*. The scar that Adam had on his side was a constant reminder of the glory of his wife. God is still at work like that, in all of his people. God is at work in families and marriages; God is at work in relationships with children and situations at work. The Spirit divides, but then he puts it back together. The Spirit cuts, and he *does* hurt us, but he hurts us like a faithful physician, a wise surgeon, because he has glory set before us. This is God's fatherly love for us. He treats us like sons, like his own Son, who endured the cross for the joy set before him (Heb. 12:1–11). Jesus is the new Adam whose side has been pierced in order for his Eve-bride, the Church, to be formed. First comes death, then resurrection.

This also means that the Spirit poured out at Pentecost makes God's people agents of the Spirit. Not only is the Spirit at work in you, but you are carrying that Spirit with you wherever you go.

Christians are all burning bushes. Moses saw a bush on fire in the wilderness, burning without being consumed. That's what God does at Pentecost. He pours out his Spirit on his people, and it begins consuming the dross. He consumes the sin, breaks us and makes us new, but the intention is not to destroy us. The purpose is to make us burn with his glory, to make us agents of the life-giving Spirit. God wants to turn his people into his wind, his fire, his word, to make us agents of grace to our wife, to our husband, to our children, to our neighbors, and to our enemies. That is what God is doing with Job, and that is why as soon as Job is lit on fire by the Spirit, controversy breaks out.

5

## Faith That Receives and Cries Out: Job 2–3

How do you respond to hardships? What do you do when taxes are higher than you expected? What do you do when your car breaks down? How do you respond when you're not getting along with your spouse, your parents, or your children? How do you respond when everything just keeps getting more expensive, or when it rains? How do you respond to great sickness, illness, or pain? How do you respond when it hurts and it won't stop hurting? What do you do? Do you just resign yourself to it? Do you yell, cry, or throw things?

Chapters 2 and 3 are a hinge upon which the book turns. The Satan has come before the heavenly assembly looking for someone to accuse. The Lord, in his great love for Job, has sent him into battle, allowing these calamities to fall upon Job. The initial response of Job was blessing and worship (1:20–21), but the greater portion of the book of Job is a far more expansive response than this. After the second calamity strikes—this time an attack laid against Job's own body—he once again responds in submission to God's wisdom in dealing out "good" and "evil" (2:10). The following consideration seeks to hold these two initial and submissive responses together with the third and more startling response of Job which begins in 3:1, "After this Job opened his mouth and cursed his day." At the end of the book of Job, God will justify the words of Job. God will say that Job was right in what he said (42:7). How is Jhe right? How can we learn the wisdom of Job?

## THE SECOND TRIAL: BOILS

Chapter 2 opens with a similar episode as in 1:6. There is a day when the sons of God come to present themselves before the Lord and the courtroom scene is replicated. The sons of God—those angels and men granted access to the presence of God—are gathered before the throne (2:1). They are God's counselors, and the Satan comes in among them again. The Satan is the accuser, the adversary (Rev. 12:10). He comes in among the sons of God as the prosecuting attorney and has a nearly identical conversation with Yahweh as before. Yahweh asks Satan where he came from. "What have you been doing?" Satan replies, "Going to and fro, walking back on the earth." The Lord again asks, "Have you considered my servant Job? There's none like him on the earth, blameless and upright, one who fears God and shuns evil"—the same thing that he said before (2:2–3). Only here, Yahweh is aware of Satan's failure to cause Job to curse God. He still holds fast to his integrity, though Satan moved Yahweh against him (2:3). It's important to note that this word which is translated "integrity" is basically another form of the word "blameless" or "perfect." Job was declared "without blemish" or "blameless" in the beginning (1:1). Yahweh reiterated this point to the Satan in the heavenly courtroom (1:8), and here Yahweh again insists that it is true and points out that Job is clinging to it.

Yahweh does not deny or hide the fact that he was involved in the calamities that befell Job. It was his fire and wind that struck Job's house (1:16, 19). It was the "hand" of Yahweh that was stretched out, allowing Satan to have power over him (1:11–12).

Honesty makes these words horrific. We are frequently too hardened and calloused to feel the horror when God first draws Satan's attention to Job. If we're reading carefully we ought to cringe. God is pointing out someone *to Satan*. "Have you considered Job, my servant? I love *him*. Try him on for size. I bet you can't get him to curse me." We hope silently that God doesn't love us like that. Hopefully, God isn't *that* proud of us. Hopefully he's not making bets with my life. Here in chapter 2, Yahweh says it again. "Have you considered my servant Job, that he is blameless, he's upright?"

The Satan responds and says, "Yeah, but you didn't really let me get to him. If you gave me a chance, I'd get him. Stretch out your hand now, touch his bone and his flesh, and he will surely curse you to your face" (2:4–5). Skin is on the outside. You just barely gave him a scratch, but let me get to his bones, let me get inside him, let me *really* mess with him. Again, the word here for "curse" is the same word used throughout the prologue that ordinarily means "bless." Recalling Job's initial response to the first round of hardships where he "blessed" the name of the Lord (1:21), there is some sense in which Job has already "blessed" Yahweh to his face. Blessing is underwritten into the text of the story, even in the mouth of the Accuser. Therefore, the Lord says to Satan, "Behold, he is in your hand; only spare his life" (2:6). The Lord gives the Satan permission to touch Job's body short of taking his life, and the Satan strikes Job with boils (2:7–8).

This is not the first time boils have been laid on people. The sixth plague that fell on Egypt, which sprang from the dust that Moses threw toward heaven, was boils (Ex. 9:8–12). Moses was instructed to take ash from the stove and cast it toward heaven, and when he did, it became boils so extreme and painful that the magicians could not stand in the presence of Pharaoh any longer. Boils are one of the plagues that God brought to destroy Pharaoh and the nation that was holding his son captive (cf. Ex. 4:22–23).

Later, in the renewal of the covenant in Deuteronomy, after wandering in the wilderness for forty years, God reminds his people what it means to be his people. Being his covenant people means great blessing if they cling to him in faith and obedience, and it means horrific curses for unbelief and disobedience. One of the specific curses promised in Deuteronomy 28:27 is boils. Not just any boils, but specifically the boils of Egypt. If Israel turned away from God and ceased from following his ways, he would cover them with the boils of Egypt. He promised to cover them with tumors, scabs, and boils that could not be healed. The symbolism is pretty straight forward: if Israel breaks faith and leaves the God who delivered them from Egypt, they will, in effect, be choosing to be back in Egypt. If they want to be back in Egypt, then God will give them a taste of Egypt. He will give them the boils of Egypt. The same promised curse is repeated in Deuteronomy 28:35 where Moses says, "The LORD will strike you on the knees and on the legs with grievous boils of which you cannot be healed, from the sole of your foot to the crown of your head." That sounds a lot like Job. He was struck with boils, from his feet to the crown of his head (2:7). Job looks like he's falling under the curse of the covenant. He looks like he has broken the covenant and has fallen under God's judgment. He is covered in the boils of Egypt, from the sole of his foot to the crown of his head.

Another instance of boils is in the case of Hezekiah in 2 Kings 20. There, God gives the king a specific word about the boil. It's not just that he is suffering under it, but the Lord says that Hezekiah will die from this boil. Isaiah the prophet, the son of Amoz, came to him and said, "Thus says the LORD, 'Set your house in order, for you shall die; you shall not recover' " (2 Kings 20:1). What is striking is that Hezekiah doesn't take the prophet's word as the final word. The king refuses to accept this word of God as the last word on the subject. The text says that Hezekiah turned his face toward the wall and "prayed to the Lord saying, 'Now, O LORD, please remember how I have walked before you in faithfulness and with a whole heart, and have done what is good in your sight.' And Hezekiah wept bitterly" (2 Kings 20:2–3). Hezekiah's response is not to let it go, not to resign himself to the word of the Lord, but to question God and plead with him, to cry out to him even in *bitterness*. Before the prophet has even left the court, the Lord hears the king's prayer and sends Isaiah back to tell him that he will heal him and add fifteen years to his life (2 Kings 20:5–6). Isaiah gave instructions to take a clump of figs and lay it on the boil, and Hezekiah recovers. Hezekiah is struck with a *terminal* illness, but his response is an appeal to God to change his mind. Hezekiah even appeals to his own faithfulness and righteousness, and God is pleased with this prayer. Hezekiah does not take God's initial word as the last word. In fact, it is the initial word which invites a response, a dialogue, an argument. God talks to his friends, and in a glorious and wonderful mystery, God loves it when they talk back to him. This seems strange, impious, and rebellious to us.

On the other hand, we have Job, the blameless man, struck with the curses of the Deuteronomic Covenant; a covenant *keeper* struck with the curses of a covenant *breaker*. This seems strange and wrong. The three friends will latch on to this when Job's response is not quiet and submissive. They will point out (helpfully) that Job doesn't *look* like a righteous man, and they are quite right. Job looks like he has been struck with the plagues of Egypt; he looks like he has been struck with the curses of the covenant. Job looks like a cursed man. This raises questions about the nature of the covenant. If Job has not broken covenant with God, has God broken covenant with Job? Was there fine print in the covenant document that Israel and Job had not seen?

First of all, we might wonder if the covenant even applies to Job, apparently a Gentile Edomite king. Would Job have recognized these boils as signs of covenant cursing? Would his friends? Can non-covenant members fall under the curses of the covenant? While Job does not appear to have been a formal Israelite, we ought to recall that he was at least familiar enough with the covenant of Israel to offer Ascension Offerings and worship the God of Israel with the covenant name "Yahweh" (1:5, 21). It is unlikely that such an understanding would have not included significant portions of the Israelite story as the Exodus and promised blessings and curses. Even apart from this, Job recognizes that it is Yahweh who has struck him (12:9) even though he has been righteous and upright before him. Job assumes a relationship with God which includes blessings for obedience and faith, and his friends assume this repeatedly, along with the corollary that God curses those who have disobeyed and turned away from him. Job's integrity is based on a rich understanding of God's covenant mercy, covenant law, and covenant blessings and curses. For now, we insist that the covenant does apply here, and we will return to the question later in this chapter.

### JOB'S RESPONSE TO THE SECOND TRIAL

Job's response to the boils is to take a potsherd and scrape himself as he sits in the midst of the ashes (2:8). We've previously pointed out that the calamities that have fallen upon Job are described in sacrificial imagery. In particular in chapter 1, we noted that the calamities fall in a certain structure, a sacrificial sequence, with the fire of God falling from heaven and consuming Job's livelihood at the center. The sacrificial sword and fire have struck the house of Job, and here they leave Job in the ashes. This response connects the first and second rounds of disaster. The fire of God has fallen and consumed his household; he has been struck with boils, and now he sits in the ashes of that judgment.

Sitting in ashes is a sign of being under the judgment of God. Remember the city of Nineveh, after Jonah came and preached impending doom. The response of the king and all his people was universal, taking up sackcloth and ashes and fasting (Jonah 2:5). Perhaps the Lord will relent from his anger, they said in desperate hopefulness, and of course, he did (Jonah 2:9–10).

Ash is also like dust. Dust and ashes are two words that frequently go together. Ash is like dust and dirt except that it is the remains of something. It's not just dirt, but it is what remains after something has been consumed by fire. Ash symbolizes a return to the dust and a return to the ground (cf. Gen. 3:19). This reminds us of the first chapters of Genesis. When the first disasters are announced, Job tears his clothes, shaves his head and falls to the ground. There he is in the dirt, an Adam, returning to the dust from which he was made. Job sitting in ashes is a sign of mortality, judgment, and frailty.

This is not all that "dust and ashes" seems to indicate, however. Abraham uses this phrase "dust and ashes" in Genesis 18:27. Abraham appeals to God's justice in response to the announcement that he has determined to destroy Sodom and Gomorrah. Here God identifies Abraham as a particularly important human to consult about his plans. "Shall I hide from Abraham what I am about to do, seeing that Abraham shall surely become a great and mighty nation, and all the nations of the earth shall be blessed in him?" (Gen. 18:17–18). Still, Abraham isn't convinced that God's plan is a good idea. Abraham asks God if he would destroy the righteous with the wicked. "Would you not make a distinction between those who are faithful and those who are faithless?" Abraham begins negotiating with the Lord of heaven, beginning with the number fifty. "If there are fifty righteous within the city, will you not spare the city?" God grants this request, but as Abraham prepares to continue negotiating, he admits his status before God. "Behold, I have undertaken to speak to the Lord, I who am but dust and ashes" (Gen. 18:27). Recognizing his position, Abraham proceeds to appeal to God for the doomed cities, securing God's mercy on the cities for even ten righteous. What is of particular note is that Abraham did not see that status of being "but dust and ashes" as entirely inconsistent with questioning God's designs. Surely there is humility in that recognition, but it is manifestly not a *silent* humility. What that means is that humility is not a virtue for the fearful and weak. Humility recognizes grace and mercy, and then stands on that grace and mercy in confidence. Humility doesn't make forgiven sinners mousey or sheepish; rather, true humility makes forgiven sinners bold and courageous. In other words, there is a sense in which Abraham could have rightly appealed to God *on the basis of* his dust and ashes. In some sense, being "but dust and ashes" *qualified* Abraham to speak. God had chosen him, by all rights a pile of dust and ashes, but it was God's choice, God's grace, and God's wisdom, and given that, it was fully right and proper for Abraham to argue from that basis. Job will initially sit in silence in his dust and ashes (2:13), but he will not remain silent forever. His place in the dust and ashes is not inconsistent with questioning God's purposes or justice.

Job's wife is only mentioned explicitly here (2:9). She is referred to at least once or twice elsewhere by Job, but here is his wife's one famous (or infamous) line. "Do you still hold fast your integrity? Curse God and die!" she says (2:9). She asks the question in a word-for-word echo of what God has already asserted about Job. He does still hold fast to his integrity. Remember the word for "integrity" is another form of the word for blameless or perfect, the thing that God always repeats about Job. She asks if he is still "holding fast" to his integrity, literally, "Are you still *strong* in your integrity?" Some commentators have pointed out that in the Hebrew there is actually no interrogative particle. It could be taken as a merely declarative statement, "You are still holding fast to your integrity; curse God and die." That may soften the "folly" of her words slightly, but given Job's response and the narrator's evaluation of Job's words (2:10), it seems clear that she in some way encouraging Job to do what the Satan predicted he would do (e.g., 2:5).

Job's response shows a clear disapproval of his wife's advice. He says that she speaks like a "foolish woman" which ultimately places her in the same category as the three friends (42:8). Once again, Job affirms God's absolute sovereignty to do as he pleases. "Shall we indeed accept good from God, and shall we not accept adversity?" (2:10). Job says that God is in control; he deals out good and evil fortunes and we have to accept it all from his hands. Job corrects his wife, resists her tempting suggestion, and assures her that this is all from God and needs to be received as such. Job is a good Calvinist here. He says they should just settle down, relax, and take it easy. The narrator tells us that in all this Job did not sin with his lips. Job continues to be faithful in this and his words are true.

## THE THREE FRIENDS

Job's three friends come to mourn with Job. We do not know much of anything about these men. Their names and nationalities shed no light on the matter. There is an Eliphaz listed as the son of Esau which at least makes another Edomite connection (Gen. 36:4–16). Other than this, we know little beyond speculation. They appear to be rulers of other neighboring kingdoms or provinces within Job's rule. Eliphaz the Temanite, Bildad the Shuhite, and Zophar the Naamathite have heard about the calamites that have struck Job, the greatest of the sons of the east. They made an appointment to come and mourn with him and to comfort him, but there are several indicators in the text that should already have us rather suspicious of their good intentions.

First, they have planned this meeting together. This word "make an appointment together" can mean "betroth" or "agree together" or "gather together" and can refer to God's own meeting with his people or God's people gathering together before God (Ex. 25:22; Num. 10:3–4; 1 Kings 8:5). It can also refer to conspiracies. After Israel had refused to enter the Promised Land, Yahweh called this disobedience treason and a mutiny, and referred to how Israel had gathered together against him (Num. 14:35). Likewise, Korah, Dathan, and Abiram organize a conspiracy against Moses, and he says that they have "gathered together" against the Lord (Num. 16:11). In Nehemiah, Sanballat and Geshem send word to Nehemiah to meet together with them, but they along with a hired hit man were plotting evil against him (Neh. 6:2, 10). The word is at the very least ambiguous, but given what comes later, there is no doubt that we ought to view this "appointment" as something very similar to a conspiracy. Eliphaz, Zophar, and Bildad are a new Korah, Dathan, and Abiram. By the end of the story, Yahweh's own word condemns the three friends. They did not speak right concerning God, and their offense is not out of ignorance or by accident. The Lord will require a costly sacrifice and prayers on their behalf before they are forgiven and spared the punishment they deserve (42:7–8).

The word for "mourn" or "show sympathy" (2:11) is also an unusual word. It can mean to mourn, but the first place it shows up is in Genesis 4:12; it's the word used to describe Cain's wandering. Cain killed his brother, and God laid a curse on him that he must wander the earth. The word "wander" is the same word for mourn.

He wandered, and the land that he wandered in is literally *nod*, the same word. He wandered in the land of wandering (Gen. 4:16). Later, the same word will be used to describe Israel wandering in exile (e.g., 1 Kings 14:15; 2 Kings 21:8). The meaning of "mourn" or "show sympathy" is derived from sharing in the wandering and exile. Someone who went to Cain to comfort him would be wandering with him, but the aim—in theory—is sympathy, sharing in the pain. Given how the conversation and story play out in Job, the friends should not be viewed as truly "sympathetic." They have not really come to comfort him; they are like Cain in reverse, come to share their wandering with Job. They have come to bring a "curse" on Job; they have come to lead Job into exile. This is why at the very end of the book the narrator can say, "And the Lord restored the fortunes of Job, when he prayed for his friends" (42:10). The word for "losses" is literally "exile" or "captivity." When Yahweh restored Job, he brought Job out of exile, out of captivity, and back into the land from his "wandering."

The descriptions of the friends' reaction to seeing Job may all be taken as traditional rites of mourning: crying, tearing their clothes, and putting dust on their heads (2:12). Obviously they are mimicking Job, sharing in his disfigured appearance. There is just enough oddity in their actions highlighted in the text to make a careful reader wonder. It says that they "sprinkled dust on their heads toward heaven." While the dust on the head fits, why the added detail "toward heaven"? Given that the context is that Job covered in boils, it is difficult to ignore the allusion to the same action in the sixth plague on Egypt that we just considered. Moses threw dust toward heaven and it became the boils in Egypt, the sixth plague (Ex. 9:10). Norman Habel recognizes this connection, but he considers it an elaborate enactment of their sympathy with the boils.[1] He suggests that they are symbolically joining Job in the plague. This would almost certainly be *their* answer, the defense of the three friends, but Job will not be convinced. Job will say that they have plotted evil

---

1. Habel, *The Book of Job*, 97.

things against him (e.g., 6:15, 27; 16:10–11). These three men are not comforters; they are more plague, more boils.

They sit together in silence for seven days and seven nights (2:12). This length of time has a show of piety, mimicking the time of mourning for other noble men (cf. Gen. 50:10; 1 Sam. 31:13)[2], but this is also perhaps a bit over the top. For starters, Job is not dead *yet*. The length of time may have been at Job's own initiative since he is the first one to speak, but are they are just a little too eager? At the very least, once they have mourned over Job's "death," shouldn't they leave him in peace? Assuming that Job is the one taking the initiative, his silence is the embodiment of his words to his wife. Shall we not accept good and evil from God (2:10)? Job's silence is his acceptance of this evil from God.

This full week of silence also reminds us of the creation week in Genesis 1, but this is the creation week inverted in so far as Job sits in complete silence. That first week of creation was marked by words, the repeated speeches of God, "And God said . . . and God said," but this silence is the reversal and destruction of Job's world.

## JOB'S CURSE

The response of Job at the end of chapter 2 and the change in tone of chapter 3 are crucial to the rest of the book. There are a number of reasonable questions to ask about how these opening chapters of the prologue fit with the poetic dialogues. Because there is such a shift, many believe that the prologue and the following dialogues are simply not compatible and therefore were not originally a single narrative.[3] Not only do the genre and style change rather dramatically, Job's tone and tact seem to take an extreme u-turn as well. Job goes from sitting in silence, receiving these adversities from the Lord, to opening his mouth and cursing. Job 3 is a song, a poem, but it is obviously not a song of praise. After the first calamities struck, Job threw himself on the ground, worshiped God, and blessed the name

---

2. Ibid., 98.
3. See René Girard or David Penchansky.

of the Lord. We might have heard him saying, "Bless the Lord, O my soul. In every time I'll always praise the Lord!" Isn't that what he said to his wife? But that is not what he *does*. After seven days of silence, he opens his mouth and curses.

While we know that the Satan is somewhere in the background watching, waiting, and hoping that Job will capitulate and curse God, it was Job's wife who told Job to curse God and die. What is striking is that after seven days, Job gets pretty close to that. He doesn't curse God directly, but he's cursing nearly everything else about his world all the way back to the night of his conception and then he begs to die. He's doing the very thing his wife suggested, or pretty close to it, it seems. What has happened to Job? Has he gone off the deep end? Has he lost it? Is he being a hypocrite? When it was his livestock and children, he could bless the Lord, but now that it is his own body, he can't take it. Let's look more closely at chapter 3 as we seek to answer these questions.

Job curses everything. He curses the day he was born, curses the night he was conceived, and even curses the people who announced his conception. Let it all be darkness, shadows, death, clouds, and blackness, and don't let anyone rejoice. Let it be barren. As Michael Fishbane has demonstrated, this curse fairly systematically follows the order of the original creation week.[4] Norman Habel lays out the key terms and themes, specifically comparing Job 3:4–13 with Genesis 1:3–2:3.[5] Both texts begin with the theme of "day" and "light" and "darkness" (Job 3:4–5; Gen. 1:3–5), and both texts end with the theme of "rest" (Job 3:13–19; Gen. 2:2–3). This in itself is sufficient to recognize that Job's curse, like his seven days of silence, is meant as a reversal of the original creation week. The curse is a wish for *that* world, the one spoken into existence in Genesis 1, to come unraveled and to be undone. More than the emptiness of silence, this curse is meant as a prayer, an incantation, a spell; it is meant with all the passion, agony, and efficacy possi-

---

4. Michael Fishbane, "Jeremiah IV 23–26 and Job III 3—13: A Recovered Use of the Creation Pattern," *Vetus Testamentum* 21, No. 2 (April 1971), 151–67.

5. Habel, 104.

ble. It corresponds not only thematically to the original creation week but is meant to appeal to the same power of speech as the original creation.[6] This is evidenced in Job's cry, "Let there be darkness!" in exact contradiction of the first utterance of creation, "Let there be light." The rest of the sequence continues with similar correlations: Job mentions God "above" which is similar to the water "above" on the second day of creation. While there is no apparent corollary to the third day of creation (creation of land and sea), Job's repeated desire for darkness to seize and overwhelm the day is for the purpose of destroying the "day," the "year," and the "month" (3:5–6) which the lights of the fourth day of creation are meant to designate (Gen. 1:14). Likewise, Job calls for the Leviathan, the great sea monster, to be roused out of his place to do his part in destroying this world (3:8), and the sea monsters were created on the fifth day (Gen. 1:21).[7] The sixth day of creation—and the creation of man in particular (Gen. 1:26–27)—is reversed in Job's specific lament that he was not miscarried or stillborn from his mother's womb (3:10–12). Where the original creation week ended in rest and blessing (Gen. 2:1–3), Job cries out for the Sabbath of the grave (3:13–19).

It's important that we not lose sight of the angst in all of this. We're too pious, and it's easy to get too academic with literary and theological analysis. If this were translated into modern colloquial English, Job is saying something like, "God damn my life, this world, everything!"

What we want to know after this is, has Job still not sinned with his lips? The answer that Yahweh gives at the end of the story is that Job has spoken about him what is right (42:7), yet he is speaking curses. What are we supposed to do with that?

Job closes this first speech with a more formal lament, a song of despair, asking why light is given to one who is in misery, why light is given to a man whose way is hidden, "whom God has hedged in" (3:20–23). The Satan had accused Yahweh of placing a

---

6. Fishbane, 154–55ff.
7. See chapters 6 and 9 for further discussion of Leviathan.

"hedge" around Job which protected him from hardship and secured his blessing. The same word is used here in Job's lament to describe the calamities which now surround him and "hedge" him in on every side. "For my sighing comes instead of my bread, and my groanings are poured out like water. For the thing that I fear comes upon me, and what I dread befalls me. I am not at ease, nor am I quiet; I have no rest, but trouble comes." (3:24–26). I have no peace, he says. I'm broken. I don't want to live. I want to die and curse it all. God damn it all.

This brings us back to two significant questions. Is Job's cursing an acceptable response to the hard providence of God? Can God treat Job like this and still be righteous? If Job has *not* broken the covenant, has Yahweh? Has the judge of the whole earth done right? Is there fine print in the covenant? As we continue our study of Job we will return to these questions, but for now we point to the examples of Abraham and Hezekiah, men of God who received the word of God and then refused to allow that word to be the last word. Their examples within the context of the rest of scripture suggest that we have to learn to do both. Job did not answer his wife and then turn around and start cursing. He answered his wife and sat there, *receiving* in submissive silence from the Lord for a week. For seven days and seven nights, he did not speak. He accepted the adversity. He waited on the Lord. If Job stopped there, he would not be fully faithful. As a husband of a family that has been struck, as the king of a nation which will surely feel the repercussions of these calamities, and the servant of the God who has allowed these hardships in the first place, Job had a responsibility to speak, a *duty* to cry out. At the bare minimum, as a man in pain, he must express that pain to his maker. To refuse to speak, to refuse to cry out to God in pain and agony, would be to compromise his integrity.

In the Reformed tradition, a good deal of our stoicism and apathy rides like a parasite on the back of the doctrine of God's sovereignty and providence. Paul says in Romans: "But who are you, O man, to answer back to God? Will what is molded say to its molder, 'Why have you made me like this?' Has the potter no right over the clay, to make out of the same lump one vessel for honored use and another for dishonorable use? What if God, desiring to show his wrath and to make known his power, has endured with much patience vessels of wrath prepared for destruction, in order to make known the riches of his glory for vessels of mercy, which he has prepared beforehand for glory." (Rom. 9:20–23). Or David sings, "Our God is in the heavens; he does all that he pleases" (Ps. 115:3). Well versed in passages like these, we hesitate to encourage (must less practice) Job-like laments and complaints, afraid of falling under the condemnation of Paul. If God is sovereign over all things, if God rules in heaven and orchestrates every last detail of the universe, who are we to question God? We are mere mortals; we are sinners; we are finite, short-sighted, frequently mistaken, and frequently foolish. Why would we speak up? Why would we dare? Given our positions, wouldn't anything of this nature *by definition* be insolent? How can cursing at the world that God created and upholds ever be righteous?

We point once again to Abraham and Hezekiah. We could also point to Moses who argued against Yahweh's plan to destroy Israel. We could point to other psalms where David cries out to the Lord with similar complaints. We can also point to the author of Romans! Paul himself disagrees with a stoic passivity to every event in our lives, and he does not contradict himself. He says, "Be anxious for nothing, but in everything by prayer and supplication, with thanksgiving, let your requests be made known to God; and the peace of God, which surpasses all understanding will guard your hearts and minds through Christ Jesus" (Eph. 4:6–7). Paul does not say that we should not be anxious because God is in control and does whatever he pleases (though there is a sense in which that is true). Paul says that we should not be anxious because we are constantly pouring out our anxieties to God. Paul instructs the Ephesians about how to fight anxiety through prayer. This is the same exhortation that Peter gives his readers. They ought to cast all their anxieties on God, because he cares for them (1 Pet. 5:7). Paul is making the same point. There is to be thanksgiving, but faithful prayer does not ignore anxieties and pain. Faithful people will let their requests be made known to God; they will cast their anxieties upon him. Also notice the goal of voicing these fears and pains and anxieties to God: the peace of God. A believer who has been struck with particularly difficult circumstances is not in sin for not feeling the peace of God at every single moment. However, a fierce love for and faith in God turns to God and pours out all the fear, the uncertainty, and the pain in the hope of peace. Crying out in anguish and fear to the God of heaven is not giving in to anxiety; it is declaring war on that anxiety. It is refusing to give up the fight.

Job is going to go on fighting for the rest of the book. Job is a warrior. He has a lot of anxiety, and as his three so-called friends gather around like vultures picking apart a corpse, Job's urgency and anxiety only grow. Job's cursing is faithful cursing. Faith looks to God in hope, but faith is not blind, and faith is not lifeless. Faith doesn't pretend it doesn't hurt, and faith isn't apathetic about the gifts—friends, family, and health—that God has given us. Faith loves those gifts of God, and when they are threatened or taken away, faith cries out to God, "Why are you doing this?" Faith is hungry for goodness and justice and mercy. Faith is the woman who won't stop bringing her requests to the master, because he is the master and because he is the Lord.

# Part Two

# The Dialogues

# 6

## THE WIND BLOWS: JOB 4–13

Sometimes days, weeks, months, or years can go from bad to worse, and then, from worse to awful. While some readers and commentators see the dialogues between Job and his three friends as a discussion of the great tragedies that have befallen Job in the first two chapters, if we look closely at the text it becomes clear that the three friends are in fact not being friends and quite to the contrary, far from being comforters, they are yet another calamity. They are satans with accusations, more storm, more boils, and worse.

As we turn to the speech cycles of Job, one of the challenges is their great length. As early as the Septuagint, there have been attempts at shortening the text, whether innocently or not. Regardless, it is easy to get lost or bogged down in the long arguments. Are they all saying the same thing over and over? Sometimes the poetry is ambiguous and hard to follow, not to mention the translation issues that we mentioned in the introduction. There are many other books and commentaries that work through the text of Job carefully, verse by verse, word by word, but we want to look at the bigger picture while still following the contours of the text. This chapter and the next two consider large sections of Job, each taking up one of the cycles of the speeches. The hope is that these meditations prove helpful in orienting readers to the key elements of these sections and fuel greater study of the text.

Recall that the dialogues are three cycles of speeches: each of the three friends speaks, and Job responds to each speech in turn. We will consider the first cycle of speeches as found in Job 4–13, the second cycle in chapters 14–21, and the third cycle in chapters 22–31.

### ELIPHAZ'S FIRST SPEECH (JOB 4–5)

Eliphaz begins the interaction wondering how his words will be received (4:1–5). He knows that Job's confidence is still in his integrity and his blamelessness (4:6), but the innocent don't perish, according to Eliphaz, because God is the one who blows with his "breath" upon the world (4:7–9). Lions are struck by God, but not the innocent (4:10–11).

Eliphaz says that he has seen a terrifying vision in his dreams (4:12–16). A terrifying spirit spoke to him and asked, "Shall mortal man be more just than God?" (4:17) The spirit says that God puts no trust in "his servants," and charges even his angels with folly (4:18–21). Eliphaz says that there is no one who is innocent, no one who is righteous, therefore trouble afflicts all, and therefore Job ought to submit to God, and commit his cause to him (5:1–8). God's ways are unsearchable, and he points to the rain as an example: if God sends rain upon the earth, how much more so does he have the right to do with humans what he will (5:9–16)?

Eliphaz continues and specifically points out God's merciful ways, emphasizing the humble who are raised up, the crafty who are caught, and the poor who are saved (5:11–16). If Job humbles himself, receiving God's correction, he will be blessed and prospered in the long run (5:17–27). These arguments form a large part of the kinds of questions these three friends are going to be asking. Job is mortal, finite, and not omniscient. Job cannot possibly be perfect and blameless. Therefore, how can he stand before God? Specifically, how can he curse when God does all things well? How can he act as though he knows better than God? These are the kinds of questions that the friends are going to continue asking, and they come introduced by Eliphaz, saying that this word has been secretly brought to him. His ear received a whisper of it from this terrifying spirit in the night (4:12–21).

Job 4:18 was a particularly significant verse for John Calvin's understanding of the book of Job. In the last chapter, we raised a question about the nature of the covenant. How is it just for God to strike a covenant keeper with the curses of the covenant? In other words, has God broken covenant with Job, or is there fine print in the covenant? How can we justify God's sovereignty to do what he pleases without ending up with a capricious or tyrannical God? Calvin answered this question by pointing to the attributes of God, his goodness and justice which can be trusted. However, Calvin ultimately answered the question by concluding that there must be a deeper justice within the person of God that would account for God's freedom to work his purposes in ways that *seemed* out of accord with the revealed law and covenant of God.[1] Calvin described this as a "twofold justice" in God where he freely condescends and accommodates fallen, mortal human beings in the form of the law and the covenant, but this revealed justice does not exhaust God's justice. Calvin cited the words of Eliphaz in his first speech where he claims that God charges even angels with sin (4:18), a theme that he will return to in his second speech (15:15). If perfect beings such as angels might be charged (justly) with imperfection, Calvin reasoned that there must be transcendent depths to God's justice which far surpass the revealed law of God. On Calvin's reading, this ordinary or measured justice was what Jeremiah prayed for

---

1. Susan E. Schreiner, "Exegesis and Double Justice in Calvin's Sermons on Job," *Church History* Vol. 58, No. 3 (September 1989), 329.

when he said, "Chastise me Lord but only according to measure" (Jer. 10:24).[2] Susan Schreiner describes Calvin's view as "although the law is a perfect rule for living, it is still only a 'median' or 'half justice' before the justice of God."[3] However, Calvin continued to have pastoral concerns that this "deeper justice" not be perceived as a cover for tyranny or cruelty in God. Calvin viewed some of Job's accusations directed at God as veering dangerously close and even crossing this line at times.[4]

While it seems inevitable that we would come to conclusions similar to Calvin, we ought to take some issue with his reading of Eliphaz. Should we merely accept what Eliphaz says here as true? Granted, Calvin thought there was confirmation of this sentiment in Jeremiah's prophecy, but as we have suggested all along, there are good reasons to have significant misgivings about Eliphaz and anything he says.

First, what is this "terrifying spirit?" If this "spirit" introduces and encourages the accusations of the three friends, we have reason to doubt the good intentions of this terrifying spirit. The spirit specifically asks questions doubting the integrity of Job, which is exactly what Satan doubted and what Job's wife encouraged him to let go of (1:9–11; 2:9). This terrifying spirit comes in the night and whispers the same accusations to Eliphaz that have been previously brought against Job. Why would we suddenly think that something completely different is going on? Satan—or another lying spirit—has come and whispered these accusations in the ear of Eliphaz.

The content of the accusation is also suspicious and matches the early discussions in the prologue. On the surface, there is a certain plausibility to the question, "Can a mortal be more righteous than God?" Of course not, we say, and Eliphaz goes on to point out that humans are from the "clay" and the "dust," reminding Job of the

---

2. I'm not sure what translation or manuscript Calvin was working from for this reading.
3. Schreiner, "Calvin's Sermons on Job," 331.
4. Ibid., 334.

original creation story.[5] God is the Creator; man is the creature. The point Eliphaz makes concerns the nature of God's relationship to "his servants" (4:18). This was Yahweh's expression of love for "my servant Job" which the Satan questioned. The Satan accused Job of serving Yahweh in hypocritical fear, not out of love and loyalty, and he accused Yahweh of protecting that sort of arrangement. However, Yahweh's bargain with the Satan is an open denial of this characterization. Eliphaz says that Yahweh doesn't have relationships built on mutual *trust*; rather, he relates to his creation purely on the basis of his role as creator and judge. God is so morally pure and righteous and transcendent, Eliphaz wonders, "Is there anyone who will answer you?" (5:1). Furthermore, trouble doesn't spring out of the "dust" by itself; man is born to trouble (5:6–7). Not only was man created from the dust, God cursed that man of dust and the ground he was taken from (Gen. 3:17–19). Eliphaz points to the Creator/creature divide and reminds Job of the Fall. How can Job expect an easy life, a life free from trouble, when he is a creature far beneath his creator and a sinful creature in a cursed and fallen world?

While Eliphaz may be correct in a static, temporary way, there is an eschatology built into the world which renders his point insufficient. God created Adam from the dust andthe clay, but he created man in his image and likeness, and created him for union and fellowship with himself. Man was created as a son to grow up into, and participate in, the glory of God as co-creator, co-ruler, and a full member of the Triune fellowship. In other words, God created man as an heir, as a son, as a member of the "family" in whom he had every intention of placing his trust. Even after the Fall, God made promises to reverse the Fall and clothed his naked servants in garments, assuring them of his plan to fulfill his original intentions. While it is pious-sounding to remind Job of the frailty of man before his creator and the curse of sin and death, this can also be simple unbelief and a guise for tyranny. "Job, remember how frail

---

5. Norman Habel, "Of Things Beyond Me: Wisdom in the Book of Job," *Concordia Theological Monthly* 20 (1983), 128–29.

and weak you are? I know better; I have seen a *vision*; I know what's best for you."

Eliphaz couches his speech in the language of love and concern (cf. 4:5), and he tries to remind Job that God does correct his people for their good: "Do not despise the Lord's discipline or be weary of his reproof" (Prov. 3:11; cf. Job 5:17). "For he wounds, but he binds up; he shatters, but his hands heal" (5:18). All of the promised blessings that flow from this chastening ride on the original accusation that Job is wrong to cling to his integrity (4:6–7). This chastening will turn out for Job's good if he will only admit that Eliphaz is right and let go of his integrity. Again, this is exactly what Satan hoped Job would do, what Job's wife suggested he do, and Job sees through the rhetoric and pious tone to the heart of the matter. Job's response does not even pretend to take Eliphaz seriously; he sees in Eliphaz a false piety and a pretentious power grab.

### JOB'S RESPONSE TO ELIPHAZ'S FIRST SPEECH (JOB 6–7)

Job responds with amazement and continued grief. He says that his calamity and vexation ought to be weighed on the balances (6:1–2). While Eliphaz said that "vexation" is the fool's path to death (5:2), Job implies that his "vexation" is justified and not foolish.[6] He says that if it were weighed, it would be heavier than the sand of the sea (6:3). It is for this reason that he has spoken wildly. This is not a recantation or an apology. It's an explanation. "I have spoken wildly because I have been struck," Job says. The word for "speaking wildly" could also mean "to swallow," and Job could be describing his words as trying to comprehend, take in, or *swallow* what has happened to him.[7] The arrows of the Almighty have struck him, and his spirit is still drinking their poison (6:4). The terrors of God are arrayed against him like an army. Frequently, readers assume that Job is referring only to the calamities of the

---

6. John E. Hartley, *The Book of Job* (Grand Rapids, MI: Eerdmans, 1988), 132.

7. English idiom is similar. Upon hearing astonishing or horrific news, one might say they are having a difficult time "swallowing" it.

prologue, and that may be included in Job's protest. The terrors of God have not ceased their march against him. Their arrows are *still* fixed in him, unleashing their poisonous destruction. While Job is likely still recoiling from the loss of children, livelihood, and physical affliction, now the terrors of God are arrayed in the form of three so-called "friends." Job's response of pain, lament, and cursing is as natural as the beasts of the field braying in hunger. Like a physical reaction, Job cries in pain (6:5–7).

Job repeats the request of his very first lament for God to strike him down. "Oh that I might have my request, and that God would fulfill my hope, that it would please God to crush me, that he would let loose his hand and cut me off!" (6:8–9). Then Job would be comforted. The three friends have put on a pretty impressive show of comfort (2:11–13). They dressed up like comforters, they cried out loud when they saw him, and they sprinkled dust all over themselves for good measure, but Job says comfort and death would be better than these friends. He refuses to admit that he has sinned or is foolish for his lamentation; he has not held back anything that needs to be said (6:10). This refusal to repent is not based on an arrogant or unrealistic evaluation of his own strength. Job knows that he has no strength within himself, no hope of success on his own (6:11–13).

There is more going on here than simply a few friends who happen to misread Job's circumstances. These three friends are not just accidentally confused or somewhat socially ignorant and awkward. If this were the case, Job might answer their concerns and then continue to cry out to God, but Job goes much further and turns the accusations back onto his friends. Job says that *they* are the fools, and he says that they are acting *deceitfully* (6:14–15). Job charges Eliphaz and company of being there on false pretenses. We pointed out previously that perhaps this is implied as the friends arrive on the scene—that they are not so pious as it may seem.

René Girard, in his study of Job, suggests that many commentators are "just a little more hypocritical than Job's friends."[8] Specifically, Girard says that readers frequently fail to listen to what Job actually says in his responses to the three friends. He constantly accuses the three friends of deceit and lies, and then turns and insists that large portions of the rest of his community have turned on him. Job "does not succeed in making his commentators, outside the text, understand him any better than those who question him within the text . . . no one takes any notice of what he says."[9] Not only are we frequently poor listeners of Job, we are also, frightfully, too kind to his enemies. We mentally soften the words of the three friends (they quote Bible verses after all), and we silently grimace at Job's harsh words. We give the three friends a free pass and sidle up to Job to ask him if all that cursing is really that necessary.

Part of the reason we don't hear the insolence in Eliphaz is because Job has been struck down. Job's entire household has been destroyed, his livelihood has been demolished, and now Job has been struck with the boils of Egypt and is sitting in the ashes with torn clothes. Job looks like a street bum. He looks like a beggar in a third world landfill. He doesn't look like a *king*. Not only is there something in Job's appearance that turns us off, but even his words are startling, abrupt, and appear rash and undisciplined. He sounds a bit mad, almost raving, screaming; he doesn't sound like a *king*.

However, Job *is* a king. Job is "the greatest of the sons of the East" (1:3). Job is a Solomon, but instead of being in a position to teach, judge, or bestow wisdom and instruction, three "prostitutes" have come before him not to receive instruction and judgment but rather to give a few pointers to their political rival, who now sits before them in rags and misery. This also means that if Job is a Solomon-like character who has truly been blessed with wisdom and faithfulness, then we should expect to find Job brandishing that wisdom, looking for a way to answer these three "prostitutes"

---

8. René Girard, tr. Yvonne Freccero, *Job the Victim of his People* (Stanford, CA: Stanford University Press, 1987), 7.
9. Ibid., 7.

gathered in his court. How will he silence their bickering, their argument, and their accusations?

Job's first speech in response to Eliphaz openly declares that the three friends are wrong and that they are being evil toward him (6:14–15, 27). Job says that they have come deceitfully. Perhaps they had been his counselors at one time; perhaps they were merely contemporary political rulers with whom he had shared diplomatic relations. Regardless, it is important to point out that these are not mere fishing buddies that Job palled around with. These are princes, nobility, political officeholders, the sort of people that kings consort with. This means that they *know* what they're doing. "My brothers are treacherous as a torrent-bed, as torrential streams that pass away, which are dark with ice, and where the snow hides itself. When they melt, they disappear; when it is hot, they vanish from their place" (6:15–17). He charges the three men with being fair-weather friends at best, and at worst he means that they are completely untrustworthy. They know how to play the game of politics; they know how to ride the waves of power and influence. They are rivers that flow where it's smooth and easygoing, and they quickly disappear and dry up when they spot a better opportunity. They are slick, and when anyone looks for them or counts on them, they are sure to be gone (6:19–20). Clearly, at the very least Job is saying that Eliphaz is not a real friend. A real friend could be found when he is in agony.

Job says that they are being motivated by fear (6:21). What are they afraid of? Consider again the context. If Job is a Solomon, the head of the greatest kingdom of the east in his day, then the series of calamities that have struck Job have struck at the political, economic, and social order of their world. It is easy to imagine numerous fears rising like columns of smoke over the devastated house of Job. Are there other political or military enemies that will seize this opportunity to strike the region in its weakness? We do not even need to *imagine* this. The Sabeans and the Chaldeans have just lead raids on the flocks of Job, leaving many men dead (1:15, 17). The crash of Job's house was likely to cause significant repercussions in the rest of his kingdom and the surrounding regions. The friends may have feared this, and it may be that the repercussions were already being felt. René Girard suggests that the entire community was in the process of turning into something like an angry lynch mob.[10] Were there riots and protests in the streets? In one of his later speeches, Job says that he has become detested by *everyone* in his kingdom (19:13–19). Presumably, the friends are afraid for the kingdom. If they are lesser magistrates from the surrounding regions, and they see the king suddenly leveled by the hand of God, maybe they have gathered together to contain the political fallout. "How can we spin this in the press to put the people at ease?" Whether they want the kingdom for themselves, or whether they are merely like Pilate and afraid of the crowds, willing to do whatever is expedient, Job knows that they are no friends. Job has never asked for their help before (6:22–23), and while he is genuinely open to honest instruction and counsel (6:24), the arguing of Eliphaz is empty (6:25).

It is no accident that Job says their words are "wind" (6:26). "Do you think that you can reprove words, when the speech of a despairing man is wind?" The Hebrew is a little more ambiguous than this translation, and the "wind" may refer to the words of Job or the words of the friends. And structurally, "wind" is parallel with the word "reprove," suggesting that their "reproof" is the "wind" that is gusting over Job, the "despairing man." Job says that they are the kind of men who would not hesitate to kill an orphan (6:27), and in this case, Job is the weak one, the despairing one, alone and defenseless. He is the orphan, the fatherless they ought to be defending and comforting, but instead he says they are digging a grave for their friend. Job says in no uncertain terms that Eliphaz and his friends have come in order to *kill him*. They have come to *bury* him.

Job says his friends have come against him like an oppressive "wind," and that should reminds us of the "great wind" that struck the house Job's children were feasting in (1:19). That *ruach*, that Spirit-wind, came against the four corners of the house and broke it

---

10. Ibid., 25–26.

down and his children were killed. The wind is still blowing, but the wind is the three friends and their words.

Job says he knows that his days have all been appointed by God and they will be few, and therefore it is right for him to speak out of his anguish while he still lives (7:1–11). In particular, Job longs for death, like a man in the field who longs for the "shade" (7:2). He refers perhaps literally to his cracked skin, the disease of boils that has broken out in his body, but he adds to this "worms and dust" (7:5). This reference is one of the origins of various Latin and German charms against worms invoking Job from the middle ages.[11] This is also an implicit response to the three friends who threw dust on their heads "toward heaven" like the Egyptian plague (2:12). Likewise, Eliphaz has just reminded Job that man is dust (4:19) and that trouble springs out of the dust because of the curse on man—"man is born to trouble" (5:6–7). This "dust" is the dust of death, the dust of mourning, the dust of Job's frailty, but all the "dust" of the three friends is caked on Job's cracked and worm-infested skin. In other words, Job is suggesting that his three friends *are* the worms infesting his flesh. The boils have burst his skin, and they are worms who have shown up just in time for the "feast."

Job cries out, reminding his friends that his life is but "wind/breath" (7:7), that he will soon disappear like a cloud in the sky (7:9–10). It is for this reason that he will not close his mouth. He will speak in the bitterness of his soul, in the distress of his "wind/spirit" (7:11).

Job asks his friends if he is the "sea" or a "sea dragon" that they are guarding him (7:12). At the center of Job's initial curse in chapter 3, he called for Leviathan, the sea dragon, to be unleashed to destroy the world (3:8). Here, his question is about the kind of threat he poses to the friends and the rest of the community. The word here for "sea dragon" is the same as the "great sea creatures" that were created on the fifth day of creation (Gen. 1:21), and in Isaiah, Leviathan is identified as one of these "sea dragons" (Is. 27:1).

---

11. See Lawrence L. Besserman, *The Legend of Job in the Middle Ages* (Cambridge, MA: Harvard University Press, 1979), 65.

In Psalm 74, David says that when Yahweh led Israel out of Egypt through the Red Sea, he broke the heads of the sea monsters on the waters and crushed the heads of Leviathan (Ps. 74:13–14). While many commentators immediately turn to Canaanite mythology here to supply details for understanding, there is a great deal to be gathered from the Scriptures on this theme.

Frequently, the sea dragon is seen as a mythological symbol of chaos. Along with the sea itself, the sea dragon symbolized forces of nature beyond the control of man driving the order of creation and nature back into a primordial disorder. This is based on a pagan understanding of nature, whether by the ancient pagans or the modern ones, and the Bible clearly presents the sea dragon as one of the creatures that God created, even one of the sea creatures that God commanded Adam to rule over (Gen. 1:26). Adam sinned, however, and rather than ruling over the dragons, he listened to the voice of his wife and the voice of a particularly crafty dragon and fell into sin. Following that sin, God promised that history would be filled with the story of a great conflict between the seed of the dragon and the seed of the woman (Gen. 3:15). This means that history, according to Genesis 3:15, is filled with dragons and dragon slayers. In this sense, sea dragons do not represent impersonal forces of chaos; they represent people, evil sons of the devil, the seed of the dragon. This is why Pharaoh is described as a sea dragon in Ezekiel (Ezek. 29:3; 32:2), as is Nebuchadnezzar, the king of Babylon (Jer. 51:34). The mythology is correct to see the trajectory toward chaos, but incorrect to miss the personal and human agents of these tendencies. It is sin that lurches toward chaos, rebellion against the word of God that longs for nothingness to overtake and submerge God's creation. These "sea dragons" are not faceless forces; they are evil, bloodthirsty rulers who personally seek to destroy the order of God's world. They are sons of the first dragon who reject God's word, who rebel against his creation, and in their pride and lust for power seek to pull the world down into the primordial waters, back into the formlessness and emptiness and darkness before creation occurred (cf. Gen. 1:2). In other words, the "sea monsters" and "leviathan" whose heads were broken on the sea in Psalm 74 are clearly Pharaoh and his army, dead on the sea shore, made "food for the creatures of the wilderness" (Ps. 74:14).

This makes sense of Job's initial call for Leviathan in his curse in chapter 3. There, Job was pleading for curses to be uttered that would "rouse up Leviathan" (3:8), which appears to be a poetic and apocalyptic way of wishing that a Balak might convince a Balaam to utter curses that empower him to defeat the nation of Israel (cf. Num. 22–24). Job prayed that a foreign enemy might have come and destroyed his kingdom before he was even born, preventing him from living through the current calamities.

Here, Job says that the three friends have gathered around him like a boat full of mad whalers. They are crazed and angry Ahabs with their harpoons aimed at Job, their Moby Dick, as though he is a Pharaoh, a Nebuchadnezzar, an evil tyrant-sea monster set on destroying their world.

### A Digression on Poetry

These dialogues in Job are very high poetry. A number of commentators make the point that Job is some of the highest poetry in the Old Testament, some of the highest lyrical verse in all of Hebrew literature. Part of that beauty is evident in the multiple layers of meaning. Like all high poetry, allusions, implications, and suggestions can pile in to a few well-chosen, carefully-placed words. The poetry in Job is no exception. One example of this is in Job's speeches, where there is uncertainty to whom Job is speaking. At the end of chapter 7, Job says, "What is man that you should exalt him, that you should set your heart on him, that you should visit him every morning?" This highly ironic revision of Psalm 8 we might naturally assume is directed at God, but it flows right out of 7:15–16, "You scare me with dreams and terrify me with visions, so that I would choose strangling and death rather than my bones. I loathe my life, I would not live forever, let me alone." It seems undeniable that he was talking to Eliphaz, the one who was just talking about terrifying visions and dreams (cf. 4:12ff). When Job cries out, "What is man, that you make so much of him, and that you set your heart on him, visit him every morning and test him every moment?" (7:17–18), is he still speaking to Eliphaz, or has he turned his prayer toward God? Job may be asking why Eliphaz is making such a big deal about him. Why is Eliphaz testing Job? Job may be asking why Eliphaz will not leave him alone (7:19). If he has sinned against Eliphaz, he is open to correction (7:20). Job will even ask for forgiveness, but these accusations have got to stop or he will die (7:21).

Even if Job is actually speaking to God in these verses, the point is underlined by the poetic ambiguity. Just as God's "hand" has played a part in the first two episodes testing Job's integrity, Yahweh's hand should still be seen behind these scenes (cf. 12:9). When Job responds to the three friends, there is some sense in which he is also simultaneously responding to Yahweh. Conversely, Job's speeches grow increasingly explicit in their address of Yahweh, but we should not lose sight of the presence of the three friends. The friends are more raiding bands, more fire, more wind, more boils, all the "arrows of the Almighty" (6:4).

### BILDAD'S FIRST SPEECH (JOB 8)

Bildad the Shuhite is the second friend who speaks in the cycles of speeches (8:1). He joins the conversation and immediately accuses Job of being full of hot air. "How long will you say these things, and the words of your mouth be a great wind?" (8:2). We cannot allow this accusation to pass without once more noting how the "wind" continues to blow.

"Does God pervert justice? Or does the Almighty pervert the right? If your children have sinned against him, he has delivered them into the hand of their transgression" (8:3–4). Bildad is not particularly gentle. He begins by insulting Job's speech as worthless wind and turns on Job's children. Bildad says, "Look, if your kids died, it's obviously because they sinned. Get over it." The graves of his children are only a week old, and Bildad twists the dagger in Job's side. In the sequence of insults there is also the insinuation that Job's big mouth is the cause of their death. Bildad says that

Job's words are a "great wind," the same as that which struck his son's house and killed his children. Job is running his mouth now, and Bildad suggests that this is what brought all these calamities in the first place. So shut up, Job.

However, we know this accusation is not true on a couple of counts. First, with regard to Job's leadership and care for his children, the prologue contradicts Bildad. Job offered sacrifices for his sons; Job made intercession for his children in case they might have sinned (1:5). This contradiction is highlighted by the author in the word for "delivered" (8:4). The same word is used when Job would "send" for his children and sanctify them and offer sacrifices according to their number (1:5). Second, the "great wind" that struck the house Job's children were feasting in was brought about by the hand of the Satan permitted by the hand of Yahweh. It was not punishment for Job's sin or the sin of his children. The prologue goes out of its way to emphasize that Job's words were without sin (1:22, 2:10). Bildad is harsh and direct in his accusations and remains harsh throughout his speeches.

If Job would just seek God, he would awake for him and bless him (8:5–6). Bildad condescendingly assures Job that his "small beginnings" might be turned into "greatness" (8:7). We should not forget the greatness of Job that was underlined in the prologue. Bildad is speaking to his superior as though he were an inferior. This is a thinly disguised insult, which as Norman Habel points out, ironically comes true (42:12).[12] By the end of the story, Job's beginning—as great as it was—looks small compared to his latter greatness. Bildad says Job should study history a bit, and he might learn a thing or two (8:8–10). For instance, one of the lessons Job ought to learn is that godless men are like plants that are cut down (8:11–13). These men who forget God build their houses on the sand; their houses are like spider webs (8:14–15). It is likely that Bildad is working with an image similar to Psalm 1 in this speech, and turns from the "chaff," the wicked that are uprooted and blow away, to the "blessed man" who is a "lush plant" and who builds his house

---

12. Habel, *The Book of Job*, 175.

out of stones (8:16–17). This man is joyful and multiplies (8:18–19). The point is that God does not cast away the blameless, nor is he friends with evildoers (8:20). God will cause Job to rejoice, Bildad says, and his enemies will be put to shame if only Job will turn to God (8:21–22). This is like asking a faithful husband if he has stopped beating his wife yet. Bildad wonders when Job will turn to God.

### JOB'S RESPONSE TO BILDAD'S FIRST SPEECH (JOB 9–10)

Job replies to Bildad and admits that what he says is true enough (9:1–2). Job says that Bildad doesn't really get to the point. Eliphaz knew that Job's cursing and lament was ultimately directed toward God (4:17; 5:17). Job understands God's justice to be directly related to his dealings with man on earth, and therefore his question has everything to do with being just before God. "But how can a man be in the right before God? If one wished to contend with him, one could not answer him once in a thousand times" (9:2–3). Job says that the real problem, and point of his cursing is that he can't talk to or contend with God. He cannot take God to court. He doesn't have a one in one-thousandths chance. God is wise and mighty, and who has hardened himself against God and prospered (9:4)? He removes mountains, and they don't even know it (9:5). He overturns them in his anger; he shakes the earth; he commands the sun; he seals off the stars; he spreads out the heavens; he treads on the waves; he made all the stars—the Bear, Orion, Pleiades, the chambers of the north—he does great things past finding out and if he goes by we don't see him (9:6–11). If God takes something away, who can stop him, who can say, "What are you doing?" (9:12). God will not withdraw his anger from those who oppose him; the allies of the proud sea dragon Rahab lie prostrate beneath him (9:13; cf. Ps. 89:9–10; Is. 51:9).

Job recognizes that a man cannot be righteous before God and that God's activities are full of wisdom and might. He agrees with Bildad that the resistance of the proud and evildoers is futile, and that God's ways are past finding out. This means that Job cannot come up with the right words to "answer" God even if he could "find" him (9:14). Even if Job was righteous enough to get a meeting with Yahweh, he would beg for mercy from the Judge because he could not answer (9:15). Job says that if he called out and God answered him, he would not believe that he was really being listened to (9:16). He says that he knows this preeminently because he is *currently* being oppressed by God's presence. "For he crushes me with a tempest and multiplies my wounds without cause" (9:17). Job knows that the raiding bands, fire, wind, and boils, and now these accuser-friends in front of him, are altogether the "storm" of God's presence pressing down upon him, crushing him (Nah. 1:3). Job says that he can't even catch his "breath" (wind) because the wind is pouring over him. God's hurricane has come upon Job, and it fills him with bitterness (9:18). Job knows that he is nothing before God, and that strictly speaking even his blameless record could be prosecuted by God (9:19–20). Still, he refuses to deny his integrity (9:21), and recognizes that this means God must sometimes destroy both the "blameless and the wicked" (9:21–23). This is proven by the fact that when wicked rulers rise up, no one seems to notice, and this too is from the hand of God (9:24). Finally, Job knows that if he lets his complaint go, stops being sad, and puts on his smiling face (9:25–27), his friends will still consider him a sinner and kill him (9:28–31).

This is one of those places where it is difficult to tell exactly to whom Job is talking. Is Job speaking to God directly, is he talking to his friends, or is he talking to both of them? Is he talking to God and hoping his friends are listening? Even if he is speaking to God, Job sees God's hand in all that has come upon him. If, like Joseph's jealous brothers, the three friends do end up plunging Job into a pit, this would still be from the Lord as far as Job is concerned.

The ambiguity of whom Job is addressing once again underlines the fact that Job's complaint is in some way directed *through* the friends. They are rulers, judges, the "gods" of Edom, and they have gathered around Job to condemn him, to find fault in him, to remove him from office, and to kill him. Job sees *through* them both in the sense that he sees their evil intentions in trying to get him to admit some vague guilt so that they can get their conviction, but also in the sense that Job sees them as affliction *from the Lord*. When Job speaks to the accusers, he is constantly speaking to Yahweh on the other side of them.

Job repeats for the third time in this speech that he knows that God is not a man that he may "answer him" (9:32). This repeated acknowledgement must be kept in mind as we approach the climax of the story and the speeches of Yahweh (e.g., 38:3). God is not a man who can be taken to court, and there is no mediator or arbiter who could "lay his hand on us both" (9:32–33). This is Job's great complaint—that he can't speak with God. However, this doesn't stop him. Chapter 10 is essentially a rehearsal of what Job *would* say to God, if he could speak to him (10:1–2). The way that Job describes what he *will* say to God, should he have the chance, is nothing short of a prayer directed explicitly to God. "I will say to God, 'Do not condemn me; let me know why you contend against me. Does it seem good to you to oppress, to despise the work of your hands and favor the designs of the wicked?'" (10:2–3). Even here, in words directed to God, Job is clearly addressing the friends. Job asks why God is allowing him to be oppressed by the "designs of the wicked." The "designs of the wicked" are the friends' plots to destroy him, and they are standing right in front of him!

Job appeals to God as his creator, reminding him that he is but flesh, that his days are few, and that he knows that God may hold him in his "hand" regardless of whether Job is innocent or not (10:4–7). Remember, it was Yahweh's "hand" that was stretched out in order to put Job's life in the Satan's hand (1:11–12). Job reminds God that these same "hands" formed and fashioned him and are now in the process of destroying him and returning him to the dust (10:8–9). Life was the gift of God to Job, but now it is being poured out (10:10–12). God's care has preserved only a tiny bit of his breath ("wind"), and Job knows that this is on purpose (10:13). Though Job is laid low and afflicted, God would still, like a lion, hunt him like prey, bringing false witnesses against him like troops armed for battle (10:14–17). Job concludes his speech by repeating his wish for death and darkness, his wish that he might never have been born, and he cries out asking why God even brought him into existence in the first place (10:18–22).

### ZOPHAR'S FIRST SPEECH (JOB 11)

Zophar begins his first speech not by calling Job's speech a bunch of wind, but he does call it a multitude—a pile—of words (11:1–2). Zophar says that this torrent of words coming out of Job's mouth clearly indicates his guilt. How can Zophar keep quiet while Job continuously pours out empty words and mockery (11:3–4)? Zophar says that Job is a liar and a mocker, and he says that Job is actually getting less than he deserves. "But oh, that God would speak and open his lips to you, and that he would tell you the secrets of wisdom! For he is manifold in understanding. Know then that God exacts of you less than your guilt deserves" (11:5–6). Zophar tells Job that the "deep things of God" are far beyond him, "deeper than Sheol . . . longer than the earth and broader than the sea" (11:7–9). Zophar picks up on Job's legal language and implies that this gathering of the three friends, is a "court summons" from God and therefore invincible and infallible (11:10–11).

Again, René Girard is helpful in noticing this sociological pattern in communities where a scapegoat has been identified. He says that universally the act of violence against the scapegoat comes to be identified not only as "righteous" but also as fully divine, the very action of God. "Along with the bands of warriors and the natural disasters are the creatures that are fighting for God . . . the seething crowd is the perfect vehicle for divine vengeance."[13] He notices that one of the other universal tendencies in these scenarios is the need for unanimity.[14] Everyone must agree on the guilt of the victim; even the victim himself must acquiesce with silence at the very least.[15] Then all protesting voices are silenced; when the verdict is unanimous, there is not the slightest suspicion of the victim's

---

13. Girard, 24–25.
14. Ibid., 15.
15. Ibid., 34–35.

innocence. The unanimous consent and approval of the entire community *is* divine sanction and approval. Girard is not arguing that the three friends and the entire community were conscious of these dynamics all the way down to the ground, but rather like another similar episode in the Gospels, they "know not what they do" on one level and on another level know very well the difference between guilt and innocence.[16]

Even if Job is a complete fool, Zophar says, even if he is the stupid son of an ass, if he would prepare his heart and stretch out his hands towards God, if he would confess his sins and repent, then surely he could lift up his face without blemish (11:13–15). Then Job would be blessed, his days would be bright with light, and he would lie down in peace (11:16–19). It is the wicked who go blind, have no hope of escape, and their only hope is death (11:20). Job has been hoping for rest and escape in death, and thus Zophar reasons that Job is worse than a fool, worse than a son of a "wild donkey's colt."

### JOB'S RESPONSE TO ZOPHAR'S FIRST SPEECH (JOB 12–14)

Job recognizes, if somewhat sarcastically, that his friends largely represent the perspective of his community. "No doubt you are the people, and wisdom will die with you" (12:2). They represent the community, and the community follows their lead. Yet Job refuses to allow that acclamation to be universal. Perhaps there were some in the community that still had doubts, and at the very least, Job's own voice will protest and insist that he is still in the fight and able to keep up with these arguments (12:3). Job says that these three men are not really comforters or friends (12:4). They are accusers, they are satans, trying to rob Job of his integrity (12:5–6). They are carrying on the same scheme that Satan was plotting in the beginning, trying to get Job to relinquish his integrity and curse God to his face. Job agrees with Zophar that God rules over all things (12:7–8),

---

16. Ibid., 28.

that all things including his current circumstances are from the hand of Yahweh (12:9–11).

It is worth noting here that this is the only time in the entire dialogues that Job or the three friends refer to God with his covenant name, "Yahweh." While textual critics have a field day with this "oddity," this is yet another clue tying us back into the prologue and pointing forward to the answer of "Yahweh" from the whirlwind. The dialogues are not about something different; we haven't gotten off track.

Job once again affirms that wisdom is a gift of God, and that he does all things by wisdom, including overthrowing mighty men and their kingdoms (like his) and sometimes plundering counselors and turning judges and elders into fools (like his friends) (12:12–21). God is also the one who "uncovers the deeps out of darkness and brings deep darkness to light," and by this, Job means that God bestows wisdom on kings and nations so that they can become great (12:22–23). When he takes away wisdom, he makes the "chiefs of the people" stagger around like "drunken men" (12:24–25). Job says that he has seen this many times, and he is not a fool (13:1–2).

Job again appeals beyond this earthly court, this "trial by ordeal" of his friends. He appeals to God because the jury is rigged: "As for you, you whitewash with lies; worthless physicians are you all. Oh that you would keep silent, and it would be your wisdom!" (13:4–5). Job says if they would all just shut up and sit there, he would think they had some remnant of wisdom. If they think that they are God's instruments of justice, Job asks how they will fair when God comes and audits the case (13:6–11). If God comes and searches out these three friends, will he find justice? Who will be afraid when he comes to review their actions (13:11)? In a phrase loaded with implications, Job charges Zophar and his friends, saying, "Your maxims are proverbs of ashes; your defenses are defenses of clay" (13:12).

The word "maxims" is built on the word for "old" or "elder." Bildad has previously counseled Job to consider the lessons of the past (8:8–10), but Job says that their history lessons are "proverbs of ashes." He is also taking a shot at Eliphaz and Bildad's warnings about putting trust in houses that are poorly constructed (4:19; 8:14–15), since Job views their "defenses" or "bulwarks" as built out of "clay" or mire. While this word can refer to cement and bricks, given the fact that Job is refuting their arguments, he clearly means to undermine their defenses, and he says they are building on mire, something like a swamp of humiliation (cf. 30:19). Clay is also what the builders of Babel used, and that building project was doomed from its inception (Gen. 11:3). The kings of Sodom and Gomorrah also fell into pits of this swampy asphalt when they fled in battle (Gen. 14:10). Job has also admitted that God has made him like "clay" and wonders if God is reversing the original creation sequence, planning to turn Job all the way back into "dust" (10:9).

Between Job and the friends we see ashes, dust, and clay everywhere. Ashes, dust, and clay represent the ground to which man returns in death; it symbolizes the curse of sin. It was also the dust and clay of the earth which God pushed together to create the first man. Job says that his three friends are running head-long toward their own destruction. They are rulers, speaking proverbs which will end in death and cursing. Job has also been reduced to dust and ashes and clay (and even cursing), but he is innocent and he clings to his integrity. What will become of a blameless man unjustly condemned by his enemies, buried in the dust and ashes and clay of death?

At the end of chapter 13, Job speaks in a way that is again meant in two ways. Job says,

> hold your peace with me, let me speak, then let it come on me what may. Why do I take my flesh in my teeth and put my life in my hands, though he slay me, yet I will trust him. Even so I will defend my ways before him. He shall be my salvation, for a hypocrite could not come before him. Listen carefully to my speech and to my declaration with your ears. See how I prepare my case . . . only two things do not do to me. Then I will not hide myself from you. Withdraw your hand far from me, and let not the dread of you make me afraid. (13:13–21)

Is Job talking to God or is he talking to his friends?

> Two things do not do to me. Withdraw your hand from me, let not the dread of you make me afraid, then call and I will answer, I will speak when you respond to me. How many are my iniquities and sins. Make me know my transgressions and my sin. Why do you hide your face and regard me as your enemy? Will you frighten a leaf driven to and fro? Will you pursue dry stubble? (13:20–25)

As Job's speech continues, it becomes more and more explicit that he is talking to God. Where his speech to his friends leaves off and where his speech to God picks up is somewhat ambiguous, unless you have a note in the middle of your Bible with the translator's best guess. "Get your hand away from me." Whose hand? Of course, God's hand is heavy upon him, but his three friends are there as well, and what do they want? What are they after? "Tell me what my sin is," Job says. Give me some specifics. Again, this is certainly a request to God at least, but perhaps also to the three friends.

What emerges in this first cycle of speeches is strikingly similar to Psalm 109. In the psalm, David cries out to God having been falsely accused by lying tongues (Ps. 109:1–2). These are "friends" who ought to have returned his love with love, but instead they fight against him without cause and are his accusers, his satans (Ps. 109:3–5). David prays that a satan be appointed to stand "at his [accuser's] right hand," that David's accuser might be judged and found guilty (Ps. 109:6–7). The psalmist goes on to pray that his friend-accuser would be overrun with calamities (Ps. 109:8–19), all this as the "reward of my accusers from the Lord" (Ps. 109:20). He says, "Let them curse, but you bless" (Ps. 109:28). "May my accusers be clothed with dishonor" (Ps. 109:29). Finally, he praises Yahweh, "For he stands at the right hand of the needy, to save him from those who condemn his soul to death" (Ps. 109:31). Job is surrounded by accusers, little serpents or satans snapping at him with their venomous words, trying to get him to curse. *They* are a curse; they are more boils of Egypt. They accuse Job like their father the devil. The wind is still gusting; the storm is still raging over Job.

Eliphaz said that a terrifying spirit came to him and gave him some questions to ask. This accusing spirit is the spirit of the accuser—the Satan—and the friends all pile on. They are attackers, liars, and cheaters; they are more plague and more wind. Job is arguing with the wind. Job is speaking into a storm, and it sometimes looks like he's not getting anywhere.

Our lives can frequently feel that way as well. Families are busy, schedules are hectic, we talk to one another and words are constantly flying around us, and modern technologies only accentuate this state with texting and chatting and cell phones and email. Words are everywhere, all around us. Communication is going on constantly, and there is no shortage of miscommunication on many levels. We, like Job, are constantly in a storm of words. The challenge, of course, is being faithful in the midst of the words, the storm, and the wind, and particularly when it looks wrong.

When a spouse speaks wrongly and children argue with parents, the temptation is to become an accuser. "Why do you always look at me like that?" "Why do you speak with that tone of voice?" We look at our spouses and our children, and suddenly we find ourselves becoming accusers.

However, we serve Jesus, who speaks to the wind and the waves, and he says, "Peace, be still." He rules the wind, he shepherds and governs it, and he calls us to speak into the wind, too. He calls us to follow Job, who is a picture of Jesus and who argues with the wind. Job's arguing ultimately grows up into prayer for his enemies. As he wrestles with their accusing words, he matures, and the story closes with Job praying for his accusers (42:10). Job wrestles and becomes an advocate; he speaks into the wind and becomes an intercessor.

Christians are called to follow the example of Job. As we walk through the storm with the wind of words around us, the call is to become advocates and to speak in their defense before God, particularly in prayer. Christian husbands, fathers, wives, mothers, and children ought to seek the face of God on behalf of their loved ones, particularly where there are tensions. We ought to recognize that God gives storms to the sons that he loves. We ought to pray that we would learn the lessons of the storms, and then we should pray that God would come and bring peace to our storms.

# 7

## JUSTICE IN THE GRAVE: JOB 14–21

Christians should be some of the most concerned people for issues of justice. That Christians would perpetrate injustice is evil; that they would do so in the name of Christ is blasphemy. The second greatest commandment according to Jesus is the love of neighbor. This love of neighbors is not merely an avoidance of oppression and mistreatment. To avoid setting your neighbor's house on fire is not the same thing as "loving your neighbor." Love is an active pursuit of the good of those that God has placed around us, and a positive defense of those in distress and misery. This defense is principally in the declaration and enacting of the gospel, the same message and ministry that Jesus proclaimed and performed for the captives of Israel (Luke 4:18–19). The Spirit has been poured out on Jesus to deliver the captives, heal the broken-hearted, and forgive sins. Through his death and resurrection, justice and mercy have triumphed, and there is a new world being born through the life of the Church by the working the Spirit.

As we continue our study of the book of Job, picking up with what is actually the last part of Job's response to Zophar's first speech, we begin to witness development in Job's argumentation. Beginning here and tracing through the rest of the second cycle of speeches between Job and the three friends, Job's wisdom manifests itself in his cries for justice, specifically crying out for a hearing before God to overturn the verdict of the friends. Job cries out for deliverance and mercy.

Remember when we looked at chapters 2 and 3 together that Job initially accepted the calamities and boils from the Lord and refused to curse God, contrary to the advice of his wife. Then, after the seven days of silence, Job opened his mouth and cursed his life, cursed the day of his birth, and began pleading for God to strike him down. He wanted to die, and his curse invoked all the power of the original creation, only in reverse. Job reiterated that desire in chapter 6, "Oh that I might have my request, and that God would fulfill my hope, that it would please God to crush me, that he would let loose his hand and cut me off!" (6:8–9). Meanwhile, we have also noted Job's strong reactions to his friends in which, taking Job at his word, we conclude that his friends have conspired together with every intention of killing him.

This presents an interesting situation where Job is praying for death, while his friends, who fully intend to kill Job, object to this desire. Contrariwise, Job objects to the murderous plots of the friends while simultaneously praying that God would strike him dead. The friends want Job to die, but they do not want him to die *as a victim*. They want him to die guilty and condemned, whereas Job would be willing to die as an innocent victim, believing that his blood would cry out for justice and vindication. In this way, Job and the friends can carry on an extremely heated argument in which they both agree on the end goal—both Job and his friends want Job in a grave. The only question is whether it will be the unmarked grave of a criminal or the decorated tomb of a martyr.

We recognize, in Job's initial lament and curse, the natural desire to die as a reaction to pure pain and misery. As noted at the beginning, we have every reason to believe that Job really was a righteous and wise ruler. The abundance and blessing that surrounded him in the beginning wasn't a fluke. Job was a very wise man, a Solomon who has been dealt a series of harsh trials. Given this wisdom, we should not see Job's cries and curses only as a desperate man flailing his arms in despair. Instead, we should see his cursing and desire to die as part of a calculated plan. This is part of the wisdom wound through the book, and Job's strategy becomes increasingly apparent in this second cycle of speeches. He has hinted at his aim earlier, particularly in chapter 9, where he presents his request to speak to God. He knows that he cannot talk to God; he cannot contend with God or take him to court. If one wished to contend with God or wanted to sue God, he cannot answer him one time out of a thousand. It would never work. Job cannot take God to court—who would be the arbiter? God is not a man that Job can answer him. However, despite these realizations and the continued insistence of his unrighteousness by the friends, Job still desires to speak to the Almighty. He states the desire again in chapter 13, "I would speak to the Almighty, and I desire to argue my case with God" (13:3). He insists that the "court" of the three friends is full of lies and false witnesses, and therefore he wants to talk to God directly. He appeals his case. He wants a hearing before the Supreme Court. Job's prayer for death is part of his strategy to arrange an appeal.

### JOB CONTINUES (JOB 14)

Job admits that what Eliphaz has previously stated is true: man is born to trouble, but he prays that God would ease up on the pressure, and refuses to admit that this is a good reason to stop caring or looking for rest (14:1–6). Job says that this is because even a tree has hope (14:7). This is part of the narrowing of his argument. Job says he wants to defend his ways before God, even if he dies in the process (13:15). This is not a kamikaze or nihilistic despair; he believes that this path of appeal will be his "salvation" (13:16). Job says that a tree has hope that even if it dies and is cut off and its roots die in the earth, with a little water it will again bud and shoot forth branches (14:7–9).

Then Job asks, "What about man?" A tree dies and has hope of coming back, but a man lies down and does not rise (14:10–12). Job sees in the natural world a type of resurrection, but says that the way death erases human life makes this possibility doubtful. However, Job says that what he really wants is to be hidden in Sheol. He prays that God would hide him until his anger is past (14:13). He would wait until his change comes, and when God calls, Job would answer (14:14–15).

While Job admits that resurrection seems entirely improbable, he concludes that resurrection is his only hope for justice. Job's argument is as follows: he wants to die, he wants a meeting with God; he wants to take him to court but isn't sure that it's possible. If he could, he would do it, and he would try to have a meeting with God even if he died in the process. He knows that a tree that gets struck down sometimes comes back. Job's reasoning seems to be that if he cannot get a meeting now, a hearing with God on this side of the grave, the only other possibility is that somehow when God's anger relented, God might remember him even in the grave, and when he called, Job would answer. Somehow, like a tree, Job might be cut off, and yet with the scent of water be revived. This glimmer of hope continues to grow as the speeches continue.

### ELIPHAZ'S SECOND SPEECH (JOB 15)

Eliphaz begins his second speech insisting that Job's knowledge is "windy" (15:2). Some translations say "empty," but the word is *ruach*, the same word for wind. He says, "Should a wise man answer with windy knowledge, and fill his belly with the east wind?" Eliphaz says that Job is blowing a bunch of wind (cf. 6:26; 8:2), and he is not sure he should even be talking with such a one (15:3). This is the second time that Eliphaz has described the crafty (cf. 5:12). Where he previously spoke in generalities about how God would "catch the crafty," he charges Job here with choosing the "tongue of the crafty" (15:4–6). When we hear the word "crafty," we ought to think of the serpent in the garden. It is the same word used to describe the serpent (Gen. 3:1), but there is also a similar word used to describe how the man and woman were "naked" and not ashamed in the garden. This pun suggests that Adam and his wife had an original wisdom which was lost in the Fall. The serpent offered a counterfeit wisdom/craftiness. Eliphaz has offered a very pious-sounding warning: beware of acting demonic and be careful of those people who act according to the counterfeit wisdom and craft of their father the Devil. He says Job has chosen the way of the serpent. He has the tongue of the Devil. On the other hand, if "nakedness" symbolizes the original wisdom of man's created goodness, and Job has been reduced to "nakedness" (1:21), this may seem "shameful" to Eliphaz and his friends. However, it may be a sign that Job is in the process of recovering that original prudence and understanding (e.g., Prov. 12:16; 12:23; 13:16). Paul quotes Eliphaz in 1 Corinthians where he writes, "Let no one deceive himself. If anyone among you thinks that he is wise in this age, let him become a fool that he may become wise. For the wisdom of this world is folly with God. For it is written, 'He catches the wise in their craftiness' " (1 Cor. 3:18–19). Here, Paul quotes Job 5:12, but he is clearly quoting Eliphaz, the fool, in a highly ironic way. In a discussion regarding how the wisdom of this world is folly with God, Paul quotes a fool who is in the middle of his folly in Job. However, it is only those who "become fools" who may, in fact, become wise. Paul turns the folly of Eliphaz into wisdom for the Corinthians. This also illustrates exactly what is going on between Job, Eliphaz, and the other friends. Job's search for wisdom and justice looks like folly, and Paul says that this is exactly what the wise men of this world think of the wisdom of God. "For the word of the cross is folly to those who are perishing, but to us who are being saved it is the power of God" (1 Cor. 1:18).

Part of what this illustrates is the main problem with the three friends. The problem is not that they are constantly saying untrue things, but rather that they are saying true things and applying them in irresponsible and evil ways. They have come in the guise of comforters but have not comforted Job. They have come as "friends" and have not been friends at all. This is part of the striking difference in genre between the prologue and the dialogues. In the prologue, we noted how blessing is underwritten into the text. Where Job is concerned that one of his children may have sinned and "cursed" God in their hearts, the word is actually "bless." Similarly, where the Satan predicts Job's failure, he says that Job will "curse" God to his face, and again, the word is "bless." In the prologue, the narrator winks at his readers as various characters analyze the goodness and blessing of God. However, here in the dialogues the opposite seems true. Here, the "friends" show up labeled as "friends" though, from the first response of Job, we have every reason to believe that they are in fact not friends! Job does not "ease" into his defense. He responds with both guns blazing, but the narrator does not allow Job's point of view to triumph easily. In fact, there is virtually no narrator. The book of Job allows us, the readers, to fall into the argument, and this is one of the great glories of this book. This is wisdom literature *in action*. The text as it is written refuses to allow us merely to sit by and watch. Spectators, if they are paying attention at all, will soon end up on the field. The three men are called "friends" even though Job says they are not friends. They insist that they have good intentions, and Job says they do not. Now, countless commentators and readers are forced to choose.

Eliphaz once again appeals to the wisdom of old age that is with him. Eliphaz implies that he and the other friends are older than Job (15:7–10), and this resistance and rejection of the elders is rebellion against God (15:11–13). Eliphaz repeats what the spirit had originally asked, "What is man, that he can be pure? Or he who is born of a woman, that he can be righteous? Behold, God puts no trust in his holy ones, and the heavens are not pure in his sight; how much less one who is abominable and corrupt, a man who drinks injustice like water!" (15:14–16). This is a straightforward summary of what Eliphaz said in his first speech (4:17–21ff.). Eliphaz says that everyone who tries to defy God will be consumed (15:17–26). Even fat and wealthy kings will be dried out by the flame and consumed with fire (15:27–35). It is not a coincidence that "fire" was one of the calamities that initially fell upon Job—a fire from heaven which consumed the animals and servants like a sacrifice. The fire of heaven came down and consumed them all, and Eliphaz says that Job should not miss the obvious lesson: wicked people get burned up.

**JOB'S RESPONSE TO ELIPHAZ'S SECOND SPEECH (JOB 16–17)**
Job responds by saying that these friends are "miserable comforters" and that words of wind continue to blow against him (16:1–3). The theme of wind is by this time well established. The wind struck Job's house in the prologue, and the wind continues to blow in the form of words, accusations, defenses, and prayers. Job would like to know why these "miserable comforters" keep talking and he tells the three friends to please stop. He says that if they were in his shoes, he would actually have words of comfort for them (16:4–6). Perhaps Job is being sarcastic and suggesting that he could dish it out to them if they were struck likewise, and he wonders how they would like their own medicine. Regardless, Job says that he has been struck, God is wearing him out, and therefore he speaks because silence will not ease the pain (16:6–7). Here, Job makes explicit what we have already suggested in his earlier speeches. He views his current situation as a continuation of God's hard providence in his life; it is God who has worn Job out (16:7). God has torn him and hated him (16:9), and this cruelty is being carried out because God has given him over to the "ungodly" and "wicked" (16:11). Throughout these verses, the "he" is intentionally ambiguous. God is the "he," but God works through means, and "he" is also the human instruments of these actions. They have gnashed their teeth at him, sharpened their eyes at him, they have gaped at him with their mouths, struck him on the cheek, and formed a lynch mob to run upon him like a warrior (16:9–14). He is covered in sackcloth, his strength is in the dust, and his face is red with weeping, even though he is innocent (16:15–16).

Who can read these verses and not think of Jesus? As the prophet Isaiah foretold of him,

> "He was despised and rejected by men; a man of sorrows, and acquainted with grief; and as one from whom men hide their faces he was despised, and we esteemed him not. Surely he has borne our griefs and carried our sorrows; yet we esteemed him stricken, smitten by God, and afflicted. But he was wounded for our transgressions; he was crushed for our iniquities; upon him was the chastisement that brought us peace, and with his stripes we are healed. All we like sheep have gone astray; we have turned every one to his own way; and the LORD has laid on him the iniquity of us all . . . Yet it was the will of the LORD to crush him; he has put him to grief." (Is. 53:3–6, 10)

And to the Ethiopian's question regarding this passage, Philip explained that it was speaking of Jesus (Acts 8:32–35). Job has been betrayed into the hands of his enemies. In the words of the Messianic Psalm, Job says,

> "But I am a worm and not a man, scorned by mankind and despised by the people. All who see me mock me; they make mouths at me; they wag their heads . . . Many bulls encompass me; strong bulls of Bashan surround me; they open wide their mouths at me, like a ravening and roaring lion. I am poured out like water, and all my bones are out of joint; my heart is like wax; it is melted within my breast; my strength is dried up like a potsherd, and my tongue sticks to my jaws; you lay me in the dust of death. For dogs encompass me; a company of evil doers encircles me; they have pierced my hands and feet." (Ps. 22:6–7, 12–16)

We might still wonder—one significant difference between Job and Christ is that Jesus is highlighted for his silence before his accusers, "He was oppressed, and he was afflicted, yet he opened not his mouth; like a lamb that is led to the slaughter, and like a sheep that before its shearers is silent, so he opened not his mouth" (Is. 53:7). Peter references this as the example for Christians who are unjustly persecuted and oppressed (1 Pet. 2:18–24), but what Peter does not say is that Christians should not pray against injustice or that they should just come to terms with being mistreated. They ought to expect persecution because they follow Jesus who set the example, but the example of Jesus also includes hope in vindication and justice. The reason Jesus did not revile or threaten in return for the lies that were spat upon him was because he entrusted himself to him who judges justly (1 Pet. 2:23).

Yet even Christ's submission to God, who judges justly, was not completely silent. He had very few words when he stood trial, but when we see him in the garden, he is sweating drops of blood, in agony, pleading with the Father for some other way: "Father, if you are willing, remove this cup from me" (Luke 22:42). Then, on the cross, he cries out in the words of Psalm 22, "My God, my God, why have you forsaken me? Why are you so far from saving me, from the words of my groaning?" (Ps. 22:1). We see, in Jesus himself, a man who is struck by God; arguing with the Father, pleading with the Father for something different, and ultimately pleading for vindication. Jesus was in agony; there was bitterness in his soul, and he faithfully poured it out to the one who judges justly. Even as he was falsely accused, struck, and surrounded by his enemies, he was faithful because he poured out that pain and anxiety and bitterness to the Father. This is exactly what Job is in the process of doing.

Job says that he is an Abel, whose blood will cry out for justice, "O earth, cover not my blood, and let my cry find no resting place" (16:18). It was the blood of Abel that cried out to God when Cain slew him, and it was the blood of Abel that appealed to God for justice on his behalf. God answered from heaven and judged Cain, and sent him into exile to wander in a foreign land. This appeal from Job once again establishes that Job fears for his life and fully expects to die. He is a despised brother who expects to be cast into the pit (cf. 9:30–31). Job's friends continue to put up a front of piety and righteousness, and their earnest-sounding claims carry a certain plausibility. Job is covered in boils; he's saying crazy things. What's going to happen to the kingdom? The economy is failing; the nation is in turmoil; society is breaking apart. The three friends are earnestly concerned, but it is not enough to be serious, to be earnest, or to have "concerns" for the greater good of society. Wickedness can be perpetuated by men in suits and ties who go home and kiss their wives and play with their kids. Evil can be motioned, seconded, and passed into legislation for the good of society, everyone can *really believe it*, and it's still evil. This is the challenge of wisdom. Wisdom requires men and women to look deeper than surface appearances and words. It is not enough to have good intentions or to quote Bible verses.

Job warns the friends that he is like Abel. If they strike him down, his blood will cry out. Of course, they would not just knock him off in a back alley. They would bring witnesses, pass a sentence, and have a public execution. It would all be very judicial and official, with paperwork and signed affidavits. Job warns them that even that pseudo-justice can be undone. This is the other side of wisdom; wisdom must be able to see through the veneers of pseudo-justice on the one hand, but on the other hand it must also come to see the power of suffering and weakness. Wisdom *chooses* the cross, which is folly with the world, but wisdom with God.

There is also another level to his appeal to the earth. Job wants his cry to find no resting place because he wants it to come before God in heaven. Remember, this is because he wants to talk to God. He is in the process of appealing the "decision" of the court of the friends. He wants some way to speak to God, as a man speaks to his neighbor (16:19–21). If Job could get a hearing with God in heaven, then "he would argue the case of a man with God, as a son of man does with his neighbor" (16:21), even though he knows he is only a man whose days are few (16:22).

Job says his friends are mockers, and their deceit is evidenced in their lack of loyalty (17:1–3). He wants to know which of them is willing to shake hands in a pledge, and he assumes that none of them is willing. Job says that his "spirit/wind" is ruined or destroyed (17:1). Job's "wind" has been destroyed by the "wind" that has struck his house, and the tempest that continues to howl all around him in these false friends and the mob they are stirring up. He warns his accusers that they are in the process of being deceived, and that those who rise up as false witnesses to steal their friends' property end up with blind and cursed children (17:4–5). Like Jezebel and Ahab with Naboth's vineyard, Job says they are in the process of perpetrating judicial proceedings that may look official on paper but which will result in stolen property and murder (1 Kings 21:1–26). Like Naboth, Job is a type of Christ who is the true and faithful Israelite. As in the parable of the vineyard and the tenants, Jesus is the son who is sent by the master to bring back some of the fruit, but they kill the son in hopes of gaining the inheritance for themselves. Ahab and Jezebel plot to take the inheritance of Naboth for themselves and in the process lose their inheritance (1 Kings 31:21–24). The friends of Job have likewise gathered together hoping to acquire the kingdom and the inheritance of Job, but whatever they hoped to gain will be lost. The blood of the innocent son will cry out for vindication.

Job says that he has become a "byword," and, like they will do to Jesus, men spit in his face (17:6; e.g., Matt. 26:67). Job is a king who has been struck down, and his chief advisers have major concerns. Job is not willing to take their counsel; he is not willing to take advice; he's not being a team player; he's not following the wisdom of the fathers. He's a lone ranger, striking out on his own. As the three friends continue to raise these legitimate-sounding concerns and Job remains belligerent, he becomes contemptible in their eyes, a blasphemer, one they would spit upon.

The word for "byword" is the word "proverb," which is a noun form of a verb which means "to rule" (*mashal*). The preeminent illustration of this is in the character of King Solomon who is both the wisest of all the sons of the east and who also spoke three-thousand proverbs and wisdom concerning trees, beasts, birds, reptiles, and fish (1 Kings 4:30–34). Job previously accused the three friends of offering a false wisdom, "proverbs of ashes" (13:12), and here Job recognizes how far he has fallen. A once-great king is now openly derided and spat upon, but the genius of the dialogues is in their subversive character. The narrator of the dialogues does not interpret and allows the three friends to speak for themselves. We are not given an omniscient view of Job's heart, which makes these conversations challenging. His wish for death and his plea for a hearing in the presence of God—and even this declaration that God has made him a "proverb" and one who is spat upon—all of this is bound together and is part of the wisdom and patience of Job (cf. Js. 5:11). On one level, Job simply means that he is being mistreated, oppressed, and sent to his grave. However, if he clings to his righteousness, though he die (17:8–12), if he makes the grave his house, and makes his bed in the darkness (17:13), if he calls the pit his father and the worm his mother (17:14) — then there is the hope of the tree. In other words, there is a faint and subtle indication even in this cry of despair of a turning in the story of Job. Here we have an innocent man, by all rights a king, surrounded by dogs—evil men—being spit upon, and he says he has been turned into a proverb of the people. In this darkness, in this suffering, Job is a proverb, spoken wisdom. In his ashes and torment he *is* king. Job is learning to rule from the cross. and that all true power is made perfect in weakness.

## BILDAD'S SECOND SPEECH (JOB 18)

Bildad asks if it's really worth all the fuss that Job is making; the earth will not be sad after he is gone (18:1–4). Bildad says that the wicked die, and their memory perishes with them. "Indeed, the light of the wicked is put out, and the flame of his fire does not shine. The light is dark in his tent, and his lamp above him is put out" (18:5–6). Bildad insists that Job is on his way to the grave, but it will not be in blessing, and he will be forgotten there (18:7–18). Bildad describes in detail how the wicked are snared, trapped, terrified, and consumed in suffering and calamity (18:7–18). He says that Job has no hope of revival or resurrection because the wicked and the ungodly have their roots dry up and their branches whither (18:16). "His memory perishes from the earth, and he has no name in the street" (18:17). Once Job dies, any hope of memory Job has is in his own children, and Bildad spitefully reminds Job that he has none (18:19). The houses of the unrighteous are spoiled, destroyed, and cast down (18:19–21). This is what God does in general to those who do not know him, and it is what God is in the process of doing to Job.

### JOB'S RESPONSE TO BILDAD'S SECOND SPEECH (JOB 19)

Job responds to Bildad by saying that his friends are actively tormenting him, and they have now insulted him ten times (19:1–3). This numeration of their torments is striking, and we might be tempted to view it simply as an idiomatic expression of frustration. We might think Job is only saying, "I've had it up to *here* with this!" Clearly Job means at *least* that much, but a look at the interchanges, beginning with Job's initial curse, shows that his speeches and the speeches of his friends add up to ten. The implication is that not only have they insulted him actively, they have also insulted him passively by refusing to listen to him and not receiving his words honestly. When he speaks, his words bounce off their foreheads. They keep reminding him that the wicked perish, and Job sighs. He is not just a guy. Job is the king, the greatest king of the east, and they have come with evil intentions and have not afforded him the respect and honor due his words. They have had the gall to respond to his laments with accusations and insults. Ten insults also remind us of the ten rebellions of Israel in the wilderness (Num. 14:22). After God has brought them to the edge of the Promised Land and offered it to them, they spy out the land and conclude that they will not be able to take it. God says fine, forty years in the wilderness for you. Then, on second thought, they decide they would like to invade the land after all. They are defeated handily without the blessing of God on their side, and God repeats his verdict, "None of the men who have seen my glory and my signs that I did in Egypt and in the wilderness, and yet have put me to the test these ten times and have not obeyed my voice, shall see the land that I swore to give to their fathers. And none of those who despised me shall see it" (14:22–23). Those ten rebellions correspond to the Ten Commandments, the Ten Words that were given at Sinai. God also points explicitly to the ten plagues, the signs and wonders that Moses did in Egypt. God performed this great and glorious deliverance, ten acts of judgment against Egypt to deliver his people. He brought them to Mount Sinai and gave them his ten words of grace, amounting to instructions about how to live like free people. The response of Israel is a tenfold rebellion, a tenfold refusal to walk in the forgiveness and freedom of God, a complete breach of the covenant. Job says you are like Israel. I am the great king, I am the king who cares for you, who leads you, who protects you, and gives you freedom and justice, and this is the thanks I get: a tenfold insult, tenfold rebellion and treason.

Job does not completely deny the possibility of having committed an error, but they are not interested in helping Job, they are interested in disgracing him (19:4–5). This, again, is God's doing; God has set a net about him and imprisoned him in darkness (19:6–8). Job says that his glory has been stripped, and the crown has been taken from his head (19:9). He is not being honored as a king; honor is not bestowed upon him. Through the friends, God is stripping his honor from him. Again, Job likens his hope to a tree that has been uprooted (19:10). This suggests the severity of Job's hopelessness. Whereas a tree with a dead stump in the ground may hope to revive (14:7–8), being "uprooted" is a rather different sort of thing. Job details this experience of feeling God's wrath, of being the enemy surrounded by his troops (19:11–12). His brothers are estranged from him, his relatives have failed him, friends have forgotten him, guests and servants ignore him (19:13–16). Even his wife despises him, little children ridicule him, and all "those whom [he] loved have turned against" him (19:17–19). Despite all these things that have come against him, Job ends chapter 19 with very famous words of hope. Job cries out for mercy in this state; he cries out asking why God continues this rampage and why he has not been satisfied with Job's flesh (19:20–22). Ironically, Job laments that his words are not written down in such a way as to be remembered forever (19:23–24). He declares in confidence that despite all these things, he knows his redeemer lives, and at the last, he will stand on the earth (19:25). There is a redeemer, one who will come to vindicate and avenge him. Even after Job's skin is completely destroyed, he will see God in his flesh (19:26–27). It is important to recognize that this is not merely the hope of seeing God for the sake of seeing God. For Job, seeing God has everything to do with being vindicated, justified, and avenged on his enemies, so he concludes this thought with the warning that if they continue to persecute him (19:28), they ought to "be afraid of the sword, for wrath brings the punishment of the sword, that you may know there is a judgment" (19:29).

Job ultimately wants a meeting with God. He wants to stand before God face-to-face, and Job finally comes out and says that he knows that his "redeemer" lives. The great Old Testament example of a redeemer (*goel*) is Boaz, who rises up to save the family of Naomi and Ruth. The office of redeemer is found in Numbers 35, where specific instructions and provisions are made for the "avenger of blood," who was to carry out the death sentence against a convicted murderer. In the law, if someone was convicted of murder, then it was the near relative of the victim, the "kinsman redeemer," who came and exacted justice. The redeemer was also the one who could pay the debts of someone enslaved in bondage (Lev. 25:25ff). The principle of redemption was inscribed in the sacrificial laws as well (Lev. 27:13ff). A redeemer could come and deliver, execute justice, save a family, and save a people. The original Redeemer was Yahweh, who came to pay the debts of his enslaved people; he was the avenger of blood putting to death Pharaoh who killed the sons of Israel, and who, like Boaz, married the barren widow Israel in order to make her fruitful and faithful again. Despite the horror all around him, Job knows that his redeemer lives, and he will stand at last on the earth. After Job's skin is destroyed, in his flesh he will see God. Though Job is buried beneath calamities, though his skin is destroyed by boils, though he is murdered in cold blood, yet his redeemer lives. If his redeemer lives, then justice will be done. He will see God in the flesh, face-to-face, and he will have a meeting with God, to contend with him and to speak with him as a friend speaks to his neighbor (cf. 16:21). This is why Job warns his friends in all seriousness about the sword: there is a judgment. There is a place and a time where God will put everything right. He will put evildoers to shame, and all false accusers, all of the satans will be brought down.

In these several verses the light bursts out in glorious radiance. In Job's darkness, in his rejection, in his being "stripped" of his glory and crown (19:9) and in the midst of being struck down, the truth is most wonderfully proclaimed. The only thing Job has is certain hope in is his Redeemer. Everything else is darkness, weakness, and shame, but it is in that darkness, weakness, and shame that the light shines forth. God turns darkness into light, weakness into strength, and shame into glory. The suffering king Job proclaims that gospel of hope.

### ZOPHAR'S SECOND SPEECH (JOB 20)

Zophar responds, saying that it is his internal conflict and turmoil that cause him to speak hastily (2:1–2). Specifically, it is the "wind" that causes him to answer with his own understanding (3:2). It may be that Zophar is referring to the spirit that spoke to Eliphaz at the very beginning, questioning Job's integrity; or, this may simply be an idiomatic way of referring to his "understanding" that is simply rushing out of him in haste. As we have seen, the words of these men are repeatedly referred to as "wind." At the same time, Zophar still tries some sort of pseudo-pious approach. He says he is very burdened by these words of Job; he has been insulted by these words, and it is this burden that causes him to answer. This is Zophar's last speech in the book of Job, and he once again tries the historical approach and says that since Adam was placed on the earth, the wicked have never lasted long (20:4–11). It can look like wicked people are young and strong and will last forever, but they will not. They will lie down in the dust (20:11). Job previously claimed that sometimes God strikes the righteous along with the wicked, and he is the living evidence of that. Part of the meaning of that claim implicates the three friends. Not only must they insist that God does not strike the wicked in order to keep their theological categories tidy, they must insist upon this in order to protect themselves from Job's implicit charge. The wicked get what they deserve; otherwise *they* are wicked for their persecution of a just man. In the meantime, it is of the highest importance that they keep talking about God being just and switch subjects whenever Job points at them.

Zophar closes this speech with what sounds like special pleading, outlining the gruesome details of God's judgment on the wicked, those who oppress the poor and plunder other peoples' houses. This could almost act as a self-maledictory oath, swearing innocence and specifying the consequences should he be lying, except that Zophar is still warning Job about what may come upon *him*. "He will flee from an iron weapon; a bronze arrow will strike him through. It is drawn forth and comes out of his body; the glittering point comes out of his gallbladder . . . the heavens will reveal his iniquity, and the earth will rise up against him. The possession of his house will be carried away, dragged off in the day of God's wrath" (20:24–25, 27–28). All of this functions as a pietistic reminder of certain covenantal truths and at the same time is a thinly veiled threat. Because Job has become wicked, and these three are the "friends" of Job and the "friends" of his kingdom, they will need to play the part of "redeemers" and bring this sentence from the Lord (20:29). They are trying to make a case for his removal and execution.

### JOB'S RESPONSE TO ZOPHAR'S SECOND SPEECH (JOB 21)

Unsurprisingly, Job says that Zophar is wrong. Zophar has said that the wicked get what they deserve. They get it *now*, in this life. They get it in the end. And they don't have happiness. Their dreams are chased away; their children die young; their houses get stolen from them; they don't get to eat the fruit of their labors. Even though Job knows that they will only keep mocking him, he says that he would like to offer his opponents some "comfort" (21:1–3). This is what his friends claimed they were offering Job (cf. 15:11), but now Job turns the offer around. Job says that his complaint is not really with man himself. If they would just open their eyes and look at him and look at what is happening, they would understand his impatience (21:4). Literally, Job asks why shouldn't his "wind be short"? This is probably a bit like the English idiom for having a "short temper." Job counters Zophar's "anatomy of the wicked" by saying that it isn't the wicked per se that get him winded (21:4). It's the fact that Zophar and his friends are using this theology-in-a-can to sack him. Job tells

Zophar to take a good look at him and recall what he used to be. Job reminds Zophar of their original reaction to his appearance (cf. 2:12). He says that if that was authentic, if they really meant it, then they would realize that a good man has been brought low. The opposite has also occurred implicitly: the three wicked friends have been raised up to positions of power and authority.

Like Solomon in Ecclesiastes, Job says that Zophar is wrong because sometimes wicked people grow old and are exalted to positions of power (21:7, cf. Ecc. 7:15). Sometimes they don't get cut off (and we should not miss the not-so-subtle allusion to the three friends). Why do they become mighty and powerful? Bad guys get to be in charge. Their descendants are established in their sight (21:8). They see their grandchildren and their great-grandchildren. Their houses are safe and fruitful (21:9–11). They rejoice in their wickedness (21:12). They have parties, and they sing with tambourines, and they dance and they rejoice in the sound of the flute. They have lots of wealth, and all the while they say to God, "depart from us" (21:13–16). Job asks how often the lamp of the wicked really is put out (21:17). He says they even recognize that God waits a generation or two to give judgment and they don't care (21:18–21). Job knows that God does all these things in his wisdom (21:22), but this means that some people have long, secure, and enjoyable lives while others die in bitterness and pain (21:23–25). Then everyone ends up in the grave covered in dust and worms (21:26).

Job knows that his friends are scheming to wrong him, insinuating that he, the king, must be wicked since all this calamity has fallen upon him (21:27–33). All their comfort, their so-called comfort, is just empty and false (21:34).

## CONCLUSION

This cycle of speeches is clearly a turning point in the dialogues. While there will be one more cycle and a number of repeated arguments, the central driving purpose of Job's cursing and laments has emerged. His integrity and faith are ultimately based on a sure hope in the resurrection, a hope in his Redeemer. This hope is not an escapist hope. Job is not wishing for death just to escape his present circumstances. Rather, his hope is in the possibility of a judgment and vindication and justice; he wants a judgment. He wants a day in court with God. He knows that ordinarily, a man can't strive with God or take him to court, but there is a Redeemer.

James says that Job was a man of patience (Jas. 5:11), and sometimes commentators argue that James could not possibly be talking about the Job of the dialogues. Perhaps there was another, different story about Job in Jewish legend. Perhaps James was merely extrapolating from the prologue that part of Job's virtue and integrity *must* have been patience; but this is all evasive and ultimately a capitulation to the claims of the three friends. To the contrary, we want to insist that the pleas, complaints, and arguments of Job are a supreme illustration of righteous patience. In context, James is warning the rich and powerful of placing their trust in those riches (5:1–3). He warns them especially of the temptations and opportunities to misuse power and influence (5:4–5). His exhortation to all of the Christians he addresses is to have patience. The rich ought to be patient and not greedy or envious for more, and the poor ought to be patient even if they are mistreated by the rich. They ought not to grumble against each other, but rather, they must all recognize that they will be judged: "behold the Judge is standing at the door" (5:9). James points to the prophets who were examples of suffering and patience (5:10), and as a specific example of one of these prophets, he points to Job. James says that Job is an example to rich and poor alike to be patient and wait for the Judge. He teaches us that patience is not always silent, and it cries out to the Judge for justice. Faithful patience does not grumble, but faithful patience turns to the Judge and pleads for mercy.

Many of the same evils in Job's world continue down through the ages: the oppression and mistreatment of the poor, the needs of orphans and widows, murder of the fatherless and the strangers, abusive spouses and parents, many sins and evils that go unnoticed, blood that goes into the ground and cries out for justice. Many of these evils happen to lone victims, to the weak and helpless, to people who have been abandoned by everyone. Like Job, many of those who suffer do so as friendless and completely alone. The exhortation of James is to cling to your integrity in hope that there is a judgment. There is a Redeemer, and the gospel of Jesus is the appearance of this Redeemer. Jesus is the innocent one whom the world turned against. Jesus is the righteous one, and they crucified him. They killed him as a robber, but God intervened for his Son. The resurrection is the answer to the injustice. The resurrection is the answer to the accusation, all the accusations. They said Jesus was a wicked blasphemer and revolutionary, and God responded by raising him from the dead, by contradicting their claims, by proving that he was Israel's King. The resurrection was the justification of Jesus. It was his vindication. The resurrection was the *judgment* of Jesus. It has happened already in order that we might have hope. It is the final word that has broken into the middle of history so that we who are still in the middle of history may learn to pray and argue and wrestle like Job.

8

## CROWNED WITH WISDOM: JOB 22–31

Job is not the only good guy to have been the object of a manhunt. David was likewise persecuted, hunted, and mistreated by Saul. David employed various schemes to stay alive in an honorable way, and in 1 Samuel 21 there is one particular instance of David's cunning. Having fled from Saul, David ended up in the city of Gath under the protection of King Achish (1 Sam. 21:10). However, word got back to Achish that this David was the same one described in a song which was apparently number one on the Billboard charts that year. "Saul has struck down his thousands, and David his ten thousands" (1 Sam. 21:11). David apparently found out that his reputation had been raised as a concern to Achish, and David, afraid for his life again, broke into his insanity routine down at the gates of the city (1 Sam. 21:12–13). He clawed at the doors of the city and drooled down his beard, and having convinced Achish that he was in fact mad, he was able to make an easy escape (1 Sam. 21:14–22:1). Even in this madness, David was preparing for and beginning to exercise the wisdom of a king. The same reckless faith that held the young shepherd boy to challenge the giant warrior of the Philistines could play insane when the occasion called for it.

This example of a righteous man being pursued and threatened illustrates how wisdom frequently looks foolish. Wisdom takes chances and can sometimes look literally mad. Job, like David, is a man of wisdom and cunning. While we have no record of Job drooling down his beard, Job has still spoken in strong language, and he continues to run his mouth in this third cycle of speeches. We want to keep in mind both the fact that Job is being pursued by his enemies who want him dead, and that we know from the end of the story that Job speaks what is right (42:7). Faithful Abraham lied to the King of Egypt to protect his wife, David drooled on his beard, and centuries later, Paul was let down out of a window in a basket. Wise men must sometimes take extreme measures to protect their loved ones, their own lives, as well as the lives and responsibilities entrusted to them. This does not mean that we must give Job a perfect grade for every last word he speaks, but we ought to take Yahweh's word seriously and read Job in the most sympathetic light possible. These examples of wise cunning and extreme measures should not be viewed as "weaseling" out of difficult situations, but should rather be understood as acts of warfare, wrestling, and striving for the glory and blessing of God. The cross of Jesus is the central picture of this "folly." This is the "secret and hidden wisdom of God, which God decreed before the ages for our glory" (1 Cor. 2:7). This wisdom of God is necessarily underhanded, "crafty," surprising, such that "none of the rulers of this age understood this, for if they had, they would not have crucified the Lord of glory" (1 Cor. 3:8). In other words, just when the rulers of the first century believed that they had finished Jesus off, it was actually the moment in which Jesus had finished *them* off. In the deepest darkness of that first Good Friday, it looked like a tragic defeat for the naked and crucified would-be king of the Jews. Yet that very moment was the enthronement of our King; in that darkness, shame, and weakness, the world was being remade and justice was being born. The crown of thorns was a true crown of gold.

The third cycle of speeches climaxes in chapter 31, which ends with the statement that the "words of Job are ended." In our consideration of the second cycle, we noted the trajectory of Job's argument: Job longs for death and looks forward to the resurrection because then, there will be a judgment. Chapter 19 is the clearest declaration of this hope, the famous passage where Job says, "I know that my redeemer lives, and at the last day he will stand on the earth," and that speech concludes with him warning the friends to beware of their evil plotting, since there is a judgment. Job's confidence rests in the hope that there is a time and place where everything is brought to light.

We have noted three phases to Job's response to his afflictions. First, he sits in silence for seven days in the dust and ashes with his friends. Then, after that week of silence, he unleashes a great curse and lament. That curse and lament takes up Job's plea to die, but as that request is repeated through his speeches, it joins a second theme we might describe as the legal appeal. By the end of the second cycle we have seen that they are really two sides of the same coin. The desire to die is bound up with a hope in the resurrection. If nothing else, Job knows that on the other side of death there is a judgment. He *will* talk to God face-to-face and he will have the opportunity to present his case before God.

As we consider this third and final cycle of speeches, there is yet another movement in the development of Job's argument. Whether or not Job was consciously aware of all that his cries and arguments would effect, this series of speeches begins to reveal what faith in the Redeemer accomplishes. Christian hope and faith in the resurrection and in the Redeemer who justifies is not content with "end-of-history justice." The mission of God in Christ is to bring salvation, hope, and comfort *in history*. To be sure, this comfort is not always the comfort that humans think they want or need, but God is not the God of another universe or another world, and he has no intentions of ditching this one. The God who created this world came to be the Redeemer of this world in the man Jesus of Nazereth, and that mission was a roaring success. Christ is risen! The way of this gospel follows in the wake of this Jesus, which is to say that the life of faithful Christians—and the Church as a whole—mimics his story, a story of suffering and patience, struggle and argument, death and resurrection and glory. This is because the Spirit of God, the Wind-Presence of the Eternal God, was poured out on Jesus at his baptism, and when Jesus had finished his work and sat down at the right hand of the Father, he poured that same Spirit out on his people at Pentecost. The same firestorm of the Spirit that filled and enlivened the life of Jesus, driving him to battle, driving him to the cross, raising him from the dead, was poured out into the Church. As Job is drawn up into this glory storm and as the Spirit blows over Job, he will not remain unchanged. The Spirit-wind is remaking Job's world, and the nakedness, boils, and persecution are being turned into robes, a crown, and glory for Job.

The name Christ means "Messiah," which is from the Hebrew word for "Anointed One." When we think of the types of the Messiah in the Old Testament, we have the priests who were anointed with oil as "messiahs" to serve in the house of God. Likewise, the kings of Israel were anointed as "messiahs" to serve on God's behalf, ruling the house of Israel. Finally, even some prophets were anointed with oil to act as messiahs for Israel (e.g., 1 Kings 19:16), and all of them were anointed with the Spirit to carry out their calling. This familiar trio of offices—priest, king, prophet—is a three-dimensional picture of God's mission in the world of drawing all men back into his presence. This mission of drawing sons up into his glory is not merely accomplished by divine fiat. God could speak the word and it would be accomplished instantaneously, but there is something more glorious in the *process*. God loves a good story, and it was for his glory that he sent the Son into the world, to the cross and grave. It is the glory of God to teach even his own Son obedience through the things that he suffered (Heb. 5:8). As we noted in the introduction, this story of maturity and education can be spelled out through the stages of priest, king, and prophet. In one sense this is an eternal schooling, an everlasting discipleship. All who have been joined to the Son by the Spirit have embarked on an eternity of growing up into glory. In human history, God anoints priests and pushes them into the maturity of kings, teaches them the wisdom of wrestling, struggling, and fighting until they are ready for the glory of prophets, until they are adopted as mature sons, equipped to rule the world with their Father. God is growing up his children to become his fierce friends. God wants sons who are fiercely loyal friends, who strive and wrestle for glory and blessing, and the story of Job is the story of one son's hunger for that glory and blessing.

## JOB AND JACOB

Remember, one of the points we emphasized at the beginning of our study was the fact that Job is perfect or blameless. The word there is *tam*; he is blameless, without spot, full of integrity. The prologue stresses this characteristic. The narrator describes him as blameless (1:1); God describes him as blameless to the Satan, the accuser, "Have you considered my servant Job how he's blameless?" (1:8). The same word is used again in the second chapter referring to Job's "integrity" to which he still holds fast (2:3–9). Later, Job explicitly claims this for himself (9:21). We noted in chapter 2 that Job is one of a number of biblical characters described in this fashion. Noah, Jacob, and David are all described as blameless, and Abraham is urged to walk before the Lord and be blameless. The character and story of Jacob, in particular, provide a number of parallels with Job that are helpful as we continue to consider the wisdom of Job.

Jacob is described as blameless, in contrast to Esau, who is the hairy hunter. "When the boys grew up, Esau was a skillful hunter, a man of the field, while Jacob was a quiet man, dwelling in tents" (Gen. 25:27). This translation renders the word *tam* as "quiet," and other translations use gentle, meek, or mild, but the word is actually the same word used to describe Job as blameless. Jacob is blameless. He dwells in tents, and he is perfect.

Not only is Jacob blameless like Job, Jacob's life parallels Job's life as a story of tragedy, suffering, and struggle. Even from the womb, Jacob and Esau come out wrestling and struggling, and so the name "Jacob" is given to him. He wrestles or struggles; it means "supplanter." From the womb, things don't seem to go right for him. The prophecy says that the older will serve the younger, but neither Isaac nor Esau appear to be keen on that. Esau was a man's man, and Jacob didn't cook as well as Esau. Jacob was not a hunter; he didn't have the big guns and the ATVs. Isaac seems to have concluded that the prophecy was mistaken: clearly Esau was the man to run the house. From the womb, Jacob struggles, and then his father does not follow the word of God. Instead of submitting to the prophecy—the older shall serve the younger—Isaac favors Esau, acting as though his older son will carry on the promises and the family name.

The incident with the birthright illustrates the way Jacob continued to struggle and wrestle with his brother and with the world around him. He buys the birthright with a bowl of soup, but that's not the end of the story. Isaac is set on bestowing the blessing of the firstborn on the older son, and Rebekah, like Abigail long after her, must protect her husband from his folly. She directs her son Jacob to dress up like Esau, make his father's favorite food, and wrestle the blessing to himself. Of course, his brother vows to kill him, and Jacob turns fugitive and leaves the country. Even when he ends up in a far country with his Uncle Laban and the prospect of a new start, things seem to go against him again. First, Laban switches his daughters after Jacob has worked seven years for Rachel, and then, just as Job was insulted ten times (19:3), Jacob was cheated by Laban, who changed his wages ten times (Gen. 31:7, 41).[1]

After many years, Jacob determined to leave Laban's house and return to his father's house. On the way back, on the night before crossing over the river to meet his long-estranged brother, Jacob met a man who wrestled with him all night long. Jacob wrestled like he had always wrestled, refusing to let go. The angel tells Jacob to re-

---

1. See James B. Jordan, *Primeval Saints: Studies in the Patriarchs of Genesis* (Moscow, Idaho: Canon Press, 2001) for a fuller explanation of the story of Jacob along these lines.

lease him, but Jacob refuses, insisting that he will not let go until he has been blessed. Finally, having struck him on the hip, he asks Jacob for his name, and when he says "Jacob," the angel responds saying, "Your name shall no longer be called Jacob, but Israel, for you have striven with God and with men, and have prevailed" (Gen. 32:28). The name Israel itself means something like "prince of God." It could also mean "persisting with God." The name is given to Jacob as a blessing, but the blessing is also an interpretation of Jacob's life. All the years since his birth he has been wrestling with all of these people, these various men—his brother, his father, his uncle—and now Jacob has wrestled with God. Jacob calls the name of the place Peniel, "For I have seen God face to face, and yet my life has been delivered" (Gen. 32:30). God insists that Jacob's life of wrestling has been leading up to this point. In other words, God sent all of those difficulties and hardships in order to grow Jacob up. They were practice rounds with God before he invited Jacob to wrestle "face-to-face." God says that Jacob is now a prince with God; he is nobility. He has wrestled like a prince, struggled like a king, and therefore he is a king. He is Israel, a prince of God.

Like Jacob, Job is described at the beginning as perfect and blameless. As we have previously noted, that perfection and blamelessness are not an exemption from trials. Integrity is not an exemption from affliction. Rather, the fact that he is perfect is more like his *qualification*. Like a sacrifice, Job is without blemish, spotless like a lamb, like a sacrificial victim. The story of Jacob teaches us that this qualification for sacrifice is ultimately qualification for *blessing*. Ellen Davis points out that the Targum rendering of Genesis 25:27's description of Jacob as "blameless" is intriguing as it interprets Jacob's integrity as "attending to the schoolhouse."[2] Davis explains that the Targum suggests that Jacob is "susceptible to being drawn out beyond himself. It is this susceptibility to transcendence that develops as the narrative progresses and shows Jacob to be not only chosen

---

2. Stephen L. Cook, Corrine L. Patton and James W. Watts, *The Whirlwind: Essays on Job, Hermeneutics and Theology in Memory of Jane Morse* (Sheffield, England: Sheffield Academic Press, 2002), 110n31.

but *qualified to bear God's blessing* . . . What marks him as a person of integrity, then, is the object of his obsession, God's blessing, which he can never posses as fully as it possesses him; and his fitness to bear it is proven by his capacity to sustain that obsession until at last he is transformed by the weight of glory."[3]

Like Jacob, Job is obsessed with God's blessing. The storm of God's presence has struck Job, but it has not stopped, and Job has refused to roll over in passivity or apathy. The storm continues in the form of people and words, and the three satan-accusers have gathered around him hungry for the kill. Like Jacob, Job is surrounded, accused, and mistreated by evil men, and Job is wrestling with them. He wrestles with the wind, and refuses to let go. These three men are evil liars who are after his life, seeking to wrestle the birthright and perhaps even the kingdom from Job, but Job, like Jacob, refuses to let go or give in until he is blessed by God. His own story will culminate in a meeting with God face-to-face. Job will wrestle with God and with men, and prevail. He will wrestle until he becomes an Israel, a prince of God. This end toward which Job struggles finally begins to emerge as the arguments come to an end in this third cycle of speeches.

### ELIPHAZ'S THIRD SPEECH (JOB 22)

Eliphaz begins his third speech saying that even if Job was righteous, it would not matter (22:2–3). He says the bottom line is that Job isn't righteous, and that's why God is correcting and judging him (22:4–5). We should not miss the fact that the speeches of the friends are getting more tense. Eliphaz, in particular, started out fairly nice. Eliphaz began with at least the show of humility and meekness. "If one attempts a word with you, will you become weary?" (4:2). He recognized that Job had often been the one to speak words of comfort to those who were weak or stumbling, and he notes that Job is now in need of comfort (4:3–5). By this third speech Eliphaz is through with the niceties. He says it doesn't mat-

---

3. Ibid., 111, emphasis mine.

ter even if Job were righteous (22:3), and asks incredulously, "Is it because your fear of him that he corrects you and enters into judgment with you?" (22:4). The great irony is that the prologue of Job says that this *is* why God has identified Job for this trial. Job "feared God" (1:1), and God noticed this and it delighted him (1:8). Job's righteousness and integrity *were* the cause of God's affection and attention. The other item to note is that Eliphaz says that God enters into judgment with Job, and he means to discredit Job's position in the "litigation." Eliphaz is sure that Job is in the position that he is in because of his *guilt*. Why else do people get brought up on charges? The implication is that God has brought Job into judgment because of his great wickedness.

Recall that Job has been asking for a judgment. Job has been pleading with God for an appointment, a hearing, a day in court (13:3; 23:4). He has also admitted that there is not much possibility of such a hearing (9:16, 32). Who takes God to court? Who would be the judge? Who would put his hands on my shoulder and God's shoulder and say, "Let's work this out" (9:33)? That couldn't happen. Job's only hope is in the possibility of resurrection. Eliphaz says that Job is already under judgment, and Job seems to recognize this too. Previously, he has stated that it is God who has dragged him to court. "And do you open your eyes on such a one and bring me into judgment with you?" (14:3). First the calamities on his household, then the boils, and now these friends surrounding him. Job knows he is under the judgment of God. There is no question in Job's mind that all of this is from God (e.g., 9:17–18), but Job wants a judgment on the judgment; he wants an appeal. All of the hardship has fallen in judgment-like precision, but even more specifically, we can identify the accusations of the three friends as a judgment. They are the prosecuting attorney, the judge, the jury, the entire court, and they believe they speak on behalf of God. They are the judgment of God (though not in the way *they* think), and Job recognizes this, yet Job refuses for this situation and judgment to be the last word. There has been a judgment rendered, apparently, and Job requests—even demands—an appeal, even if it means death in the process because he clings to hope in his Redeemer.

Eliphaz finally proceeds to get specific with a number of accusations running through the rest of his third and final speech. His charges cluster around a popular theme brought against the rich, wealthy, and powerful—accusations regarding the abuse and oppression of the poor. Eliphaz has previously been vague in his accusations, but there is envy in his eyes and he finally comes out and says that the problem with Job is how rich and powerful he is. How do rich people become rich? They take pledges, strip the naked of their clothing, and they refuse to share food and water with the hungry and thirsty (22:6–7). Eliphaz accuses Job of making deals with the mighty and honorable, while driving the widows and the orphans away empty-handed (22:8–9). Eliphaz reasons that riches are great snares: "Come now, you rich, weep and howl for the miseries that are coming upon you. Your riches have rotted and your garments are moth-eaten" (Jas. 5:1–2). "The getting of treasures by a lying tongue is a fleeting vapor and a snare of death" (Prov. 21:6). Eliphaz says that Job's riches have been a great snare, and that they have led Job down into darkness so that he cannot see clearly (22:10–11). God sees the way you have mistreated the poor, says Eliphaz, and he's judging you for it (22:12–18). The proud "kill the widow and the sojourner, and murder the fatherless; and they say, 'The Lord does not see; the God of Jacob does not perceive' " (Ps. 94:6–7). Eliphaz says that Job is a proud fool, and obviously a wicked man. The righteous would see all of this and be glad and even laugh at that sort of folly (22:19); fire cuts down the adversaries of God, and consumes their remnant (22:20). Eliphaz is not even trying to be delicate anymore, alluding to the tragedy of consuming fire that has befallen Job in an off-handed way. He then proceeds immediately into sarcastically suggesting that Job should acquaint himself with God (22:21).

If Job would only get to know God and listen to his word, not only would he be blessed materially (22:23–25), but he might also pray and be heard (22:26–28). If Job would just confess his sins, God would hear his prayers and answer and save him (22:29–30). At the very least, we recognize that Eliphaz understands Job's basic point. Job wants to talk to God; but Eliphaz says that sinners don't get appointments with the Almighty. Oppressive fools get destroyed by God, not rewarded with a conference. Eliphaz suggests that Job should confess his sins and purify his hands, and then perhaps God will deliver him.

### JOB'S RESPONSE TO ELIPHAZ'S THIRD SPEECH (JOB 23–24)

Job's response to Eliphaz jumps right on his final point. Job is bitter, and he is groaning because he wants to find God to present his case before him. "Oh, that I knew where I might find him, that I might come even to his seat! I would lay my case before him and fill my mouth with arguments" (23:3–4). If Job could just go before God, he would speak to him (23:5). They would speak together, and Job believes he would be acquitted (23:6–7). As it is, Job cannot find God, but he is absolutely convinced that God is busy turning him into gold (23:8–10). This is striking. We generally think of Job as a great pessimist throughout the dialogues, full of anger and despair, but here, Job insists that he will come forth as gold. Job is still terrified (23:15–16), but he is also convinced that he has been faithful, clinging to his integrity, and therefore he will not be silent though thick darkness covers his face (23:11–14, 17). Job proceeds to outline several sorts of wicked men who all have in common the fact that they are not judged, cursed, or destroyed, despite the suffering of those they oppress (23:1–17). They should have all sorts of cursing fall on their heads, yet God raises up and brings down in a much more complex sort of way, such that no man is sure of his life (23:18–24). Job dares the friends to prove him a liar if this is not true (23:25). As we have seen before, the subtext to these claims is the reality of three accusers, three evil men standing right in front of Job. They should be brought down and judged, yet there they are, still accusing, still mocking. They are living proof—or better, they are the prime example—of what Job is talking about.

## BILDAD'S THIRD SPEECH (JOB 25)

Bildad's last speech begins in chapter 25, and it's very brief. Many commentators suggest that since his speech is so short, the manuscripts must have been corrupted. Some suggest that a portion of chapter 27 was actually originally part of Bildad's speech, but there is a better and more simple reason for his shortness: Job is in the process of *winning the argument*. The third cycle of speeches degenerates simply because there is nothing more to say. In fact, the shortness of Bildad's third speech may also be due to Job interrupting him. As we will see, Job's response is direct, pointed, and sharper than he has been to this point. The simplest explanation for the "corruption" of the third cycle of speeches is that it is intentional and historical. Job has outlasted the friends. More importantly, he has wrestled and argued and stood fast in his integrity, and the three friends have been argued silent. In the weakness and darkness and dust of death, Job has emerged as a proverb, certain of his Redeemer, sure that he is being turned into gold.

Bildad begins by saying that rule and fear belong to God; he makes peace in his high places; his armies are countless (25:1–3). The word here for "dominion" or "rule" is the word *mashal*, the verb form of the word for "proverb." It connotes wisdom to rule, skill in understanding, leading in the world. Bildad says that kind of rule, wisdom, and skill in ruling belongs to God. Proverbial rule, wise rule, and true justice belongs to God; only *his* dominion is like that. As typified by Solomon, God is the chief proverb-speaker, the chief proverb-maker. While Bildad means this to denigrate Job, the irony is that Job has become a "proverb" of God, a living, spoken, proverb of God.

Bildad concludes by echoing the question that Eliphaz has repeated several times: so what are you, Job? Bildad asks how a man can be righteous with God; he insists that anyone born of a woman cannot be "pure" (25:4). Eliphaz had claimed that God even charged angels with error (4:18; 15:15), and here Bildad says that even the moon and the stars are not completely "pure" in his sight (25:5). How much less is man, who is a maggot and the "son of man, who is a worm" (25:6)? As with Eliphaz, the point here is that God does not have the kind of relationship with man that Job wants. Bildad says God is a cranky building inspector, and he will find all the infractions to the building code. God relates formally and legally to his piles of dust, his human creatures a step up from worms. Notice that the three friends must share the Satan's view of divine-human relationships. They are purely contractual and formal; the covenant is not a family—it's a bureaucracy with paper work, checklists, and bylaws. God does not relate to his people in love, Bildad insists. The three friends insist that God has no sons, and, at the very least, Job most certainly is not one. Remember too that this "theology" is all a front for the attempted coup by the three friends. The implicit charge is that Job is not just and not righteous. Not only do the friends share the Satan's perspective, they share his style of accusations. Men are not righteous, they are not loyal: if you press them hard enough they will break and curse you to your face.

### JOB'S RESPONSE TO BILDAD'S THIRD SPEECH (JOB 26)

Job immediately jumps on this idea of justice, and he turns on Bildad sharply. The style may even suggest an interruption. Bildad's speech is so short, as we have noted, it would make sense to see Job standing up and responding without letting Bildad finish his thought. The second person singular of these verses repeatedly points directly at Bildad and underlines this turn. Job says, "So, you want to talk about justice? You want to talk about righteousness, Bildad?" Job specifically wants to know how Bildad has been just, how he has helped, saved, counseled, and declared on behalf of the poor, the weak, and the ignorant (26:1–4). Justice isn't just a quality; righteousness is not an impersonal force; it is not just a feeling. Justice is particular actions, particular acts *for others*. Job says, "Let's talk about justice, let's talk about righteousness. Have you done these things? Have you helped those without power, have you saved the arm that has no strength?" The screaming, implicit answer is, of course, that Bildad has not. One of the early charges that Job made against the three friends is that they were not there to help Job or to comfort him, but instead to throw him into a ditch. They have come to overwhelm him like they would the fatherless (6:27). Job says that Bildad is right that God is righteous, and everything trembles before his presence, everything from the depths of Sheol all the way up through the clouds to the pillars of heaven (26:5–11). By his wisdom and understanding, sea monsters are struck, his Spirit-Wind formed the heavens, and with his hand, God pierced the fleeing serpent (26:12–13). This is only but the merest glimpse of his righteous ways: who can understand the thunder of his power (26:14)?

## JOB SPEAKS PROVERBS (JOB 27–28)

Chapter 27 begins with the statement, "And Job again took up his discourse, and said, "but there's something here in this brief comment by the narrator that is easy to miss. Literally, the narrator says that Job "continued to lift up his proverb." This is the same word for ruling wisely that Bildad referred to (25:2). It's the same root word that Job used to describe his state (17:6). The narrator nonchalantly says that Job continued his "proverbing." His discourse is the speaking of proverbs. Job is in the middle of speaking about God's justice, God's righteousness, God's rule, and he will continue on this subject in 27:2, "As God lives who has taken away my right, and the Almighty, who has made my soul bitter." In other words, while Job is describing God's wisdom and rule, the narrator says that Job began to speak in proverbs. Job began speaking *like a king*. Just as a Philistine might have passed by the gates of Gath and never imagined that the same man scratching and drooling at his gates was the victorious shepherd boy who struck down their giant warrior years earlier, so too, one might read through these verses and still see a frustrated, bitter, and effectively dethroned king. Yet the narrator, like Pilate, places a sign on his cross that says he is the king, and it is not an accident that this is also the very point in the dialogues at which the friends are *silenced*. They have no more words; they are spent; they have been defeated. There is no third speech from Zophar. Some commentators suggest that 27:13–23 is

Zophar's last speech, but there is no introduction of him, and it is far better to understand the "missing speech" as Zophar simply being silenced. Bildad has been cut off almost mid-sentence, and Zophar doesn't even get a last word. When Job begins speaking proverbs like a king, the fools disappear.

On the face of the dialogues, readers do not necessarily see the victory. The light from heaven doesn't shine down; there is no cosmic, thundering voice announcing that this is the "beloved son." As with Christ, there are clues and hints at the radical overthrow and deliverance taking place, though it might be easily missed. Job is still sitting in the dust and ashes, surrounded by his enemies. The kingdom is still in tumult. The boils still burn and crack in his skin and his children are still dead. He is still despised, rejected, and spat upon. It is in this moment that, hanging in weakness on his cross, the narrator says that Job is king. This is because the power of God is made perfect in weakness. The greatest in the kingdom of God is a slave. "Whoever finds his life will lose it, and whoever loses his life for [Jesus'] sake will find it"(Matt. 10:39). Perhaps John's version of this is even closer to Job's experience: "Whoever loves his life loses it, and whoever hates his life in this world will keep it for eternal life" (John 12:25). From this angle, we would suggest that Job has been driven into battle in a howling wilderness with satans, sons of the Accuser, having previously been struck with severe hardships. In this rhetorical combat, Job has resisted every temptation to despair, to curse God, to relinquish his hope, his faith, or his integrity. Here, Job is emerging from the smoke of battle an even more glorious king. Job, the faithful and righteous priest who offered sacrifices for his sons, a priest-king like Melchizedek, was led into battle by the Spirit, and having wrestled and contended with God and men, emerges as a king, a prince and son of God.

Job enters into the wisdom of his Father even as he discourses on it. While God has taken away Job's justice, as he says, Job will not put away his integrity (27:2–6). He continues to refuse to speak wickedness or deceit (27:4; cf. 2:10), and the narrator says Job is speaking proverbs and wisdom like a king. As a Solomon-like king he declares the destruction of his enemies (27:7–10), and then proceeds to teach them about the hand of God (27:11–12). While some have suggested that the final verses of Job 27 do not sound consistent with Job's previous sentiments regarding the complexity of God's judgments, that is only a problem if we think that Job's primary point in the argument was to prove the friends wrong. As we have repeatedly insisted, the point of the argument was never really the argument. The argument has always been a rhetorical wrestling for political power. It is only here, where God has suddenly started turning the tables, that Job takes control of the conversation, and like Solomon can speak proverbs, can speak of what God does to evil doers. They are punished, and the innocent are delivered (27:13–15). The rich and oppressive go down to death and are carried away in the storm and the wind (27:16–23). This is only out of place if Job is in exactly the same spot as he began. Yet, Job has emerged into the light, and while the dust has not yet settled, the momentum of the battle has turned and Job can affirm without impunity that the wicked will be blown away by the storm, because that is even now happening.

## THE WISDOM OF JOB

While some commentators think that Job 28 is out of place and was later inserted by another author, the context suggests otherwise. Having begun to speak proverbs like a king, Job speaks at great length about the wisdom of God. "Surely there is a mine for silver, and a place for gold," and many other brilliant and amazing things may be dug out of the depths of the earth (28:1–11), but wisdom is not found in the land of the living (28:12–13). The "deep" says that wisdom is not with it, and the sea likewise denies all knowledge of the whereabouts of wisdom (28:14). Job says that wisdom is even more rare, more valuable than all the precious stones, sapphires, and diamonds that can be found in the earth (28:15–20). Wisdom cannot be found in the land of the living (28:21). "Where can wisdom be found?" Job asks. His answer is that "Abaddon and Death say, 'We have heard a rumor of it with our ears.' " Death has heard about wisdom, he says. It cannot be found in the land of the living, but death knows something about it. Ultimately this is because wisdom is found with God. This is also a testimony about the kind of wisdom that God is. Jesus again: "Whoever seeks to preserve his life will lose it, but whoever loses his life will keep it" (Luke 17:33). "If anyone would be first, he must be last of all and servant of all" (Mark 9:35). "For whoever would save his life will lose it, but whoever loses his life for my sake will save it. For what does it profit a man if he gains the whole world and loses or forfeits himself?" (Luke 9:24–25). Or, in the famous words of Jim Elliot, "He is no fool who gives what he cannot keep to gain that which he cannot lose." In other words, death is the *way* to wisdom. The cross is the way to resurrection. Suffering is the way to glory. This is the wisdom of God which death has heard a report about. This was the story of Israel's history. Abraham went down into the death of Egypt, was mistreated, and the Lord delivered him out into light and glory. Israel went down into the death of slavery in Egypt, was mistreated, and the Lord delivered them out into freedom and glory. This story replayed repeatedly in the era of the Judges, later in Israel's exile in Babylon, and ultimately in the death and resurrection of Jesus. This is the way of God's sons.

This is the way of God's sons because there is sin and brokenness in the world, but this is also the way of God's sons because it reveals something deep and glorious about the Father. John says, "By this we know love, that he laid down his life for us, and we ought to lay down our lives for the brothers" (1 John 3:16). Earlier he has said, "See what kind of love the Father has given to us, that we should be called children of God" (1 John 3:1). This self-sacrificial living—wisdom of dying in order to live, serving in order to rule, giving in order to keep—this is the love of God manifested in Jesus Christ. This is the love of the Spirit that binds the Father and the Son together in eternal service, eternal mutual submission, eternal death, for one another. It is this wisdom of love that Job is being trained in. On the other side of death is a judgment, and Job will come face to face with his Redeemer, and it is love that drives Job to plead for that meeting. It is wisdom that teaches Job to hope for it.

The final verse of Job 28 is nearly a quotation from Proverbs. "Behold, the fear of the Lord, that is wisdom, and to depart from evil is understanding" (28:28; cf. Prov. 1:7; 9:10). Job has walked in the fear of the Lord, and though the path has been full of suffering and pain, it is the way of wisdom. Just in case we missed it the first time, the narrator once again reminds the readers and hearers of what Job is doing. "And Job again took up his discourse, and said" (29:1). Job lifts up his *proverb* and proceeds to speak like a king. We noted previously that the word here for "discourse" is usually translated "proverb" (Prov. 1:1; 1:6; 10:1) and it is associated with ruling and more specifically, ruling in wisdom (Prov. 10:24; 16:32; 17:2). The only other place where this word is translated differently than "proverb" or "parable" or "rule" is in Numbers 23–24 in the story of Balaam and Balak, king of Moab. On the surface this seems odd since Balaam was hired by the king of Moab to curse the nation of Israel, but then, that is exactly what makes the connection so fascinating. The story of Balaam is all about whether Balaam can *curse* Israel. He tries three times to offer sacrifices and proclaim a curse, and three times it comes out as a prolific and glorious blessing, just as the characters throughout the prologue speak about "cursing" but every time they do so, it comes out literally as "blessing." Throughout that episode in Numbers 23–24, Balaam repeatedly "lifts up his proverb and says." In context this fits with the prophet's attempt to "sing" a curse against God's people. This is a dark saying; an incantation of sorts. It is meant to be a spell, a deep magic and wisdom that breaks the blessing on God's people. Repeatedly, this attempt at dark magic comes out as *proverbs*, as true wisdom and the blessing of God on his people. Here in Job the story has centered on the relationship that God has with Job and, by analogy, to all of humanity. Does God love his people like his own children? Are his blessings really meant to bless, or is the relationship a dry, legal contract with various goods and services exchanged? Job proves that the covenant bond he shares with God is a covenant of love, real interaction, and true friendship. Job is growing up into the wisdom of God his Father. Here, nearing the climax of the story, Job begins speaking in proverbs, parables, and in the language of a wise and blessed king. The Satan has tried to get Job to curse God, but while Job has not been afraid to appeal to God, to argue and wrestle with God, it has all been ultimately in the madness of love. Job is a lively and broken-hearted lover, but never a sickly or selfish suicidal person. It was this love that drove Job to bless Yahweh in the beginning, it was this love, offended and burning, that caused Job to cry out in pain and agony surrounded by his enemies, and it is this same love bursting out in praise of the wisdom of God at the end.

Job's kingly discourse continues recalling his own story. "Oh, that I were as in the months of old, as in the days when God watched over me, when his lamp shone upon my head, and by his light I walked through darkness, as I was in my prime, when the friendship of God was upon my tent, when the Almighty was yet with me, when my children were all around me" (29:2–5). Job emerges as a king, light emerges in the darkness, but Job is not yet satisfied. He is hungry for blessing and glory, and he looks back and remembers when God's friendship was obvious by looking at his household (29:6). Job remembers how he was respected (29:7–11), specifically because he delivered the poor and the fatherless: he was the eyes to the blind, the feet to the lame, father to the needy, and the avenger of injustice (29:12–17). Job recalls how he reigned as an extremely blessed king (29:18–25), but he recognizes that things have changed dramatically. Now the lowest class of men, those whose fathers he wouldn't even put with the dogs of his flock, laugh at him and make him the subject of their songs (30:1–9). They spit when they see him, and they do not even pretend to respect him (30:10–11).

As we have suggested earlier in our study, Job implies here that the damage done to the broader community by Eliphaz, Bildad, and Zophar is pretty extensive. Their accusations have gotten air time on the talk shows and news syndicates. Now even the homeless and the thugs are singing songs about his downfall. There is no restraint, and the rabble is on the rise and they are plotting against Job (30:12–14). "Terrors are turned on me, my honor is pursued as by the wind, and my prosperity has passed away like a cloud" (30:15).

Again, Job sees all of this as a great storm, the Spirit-wind—*ruach*—blowing over him. His bones are racked, the pain gnaws at him, and he is disfigured (30:16–18). Job again recognizes that God is ultimately the one behind this insurrection. God has cast him into the mire, and has made him like "dust and ashes" (30:19). Here it is interesting that the word for this comparison, translated as "become like," is not the usual word for "like" or "as." The word is a form of the word for "proverb." It's almost as if the narrator wanted us to pay attention to this theme. Job literally says that he has become a "proverb of dust and ashes."

The text continues to underline and imply and impose (even upon Job) the conclusion that as God has reduced him to a proverb of dust and ashes, Job has begun speaking proverbs. Given the royal connotations of the word, we might even translate Job's conclusion as becoming a "king of dust and ashes" or a "king in the dust and ashes." He begins speaking like a Solomon while still in his weakness; he speaks wisdom and rules from the dust and the ashes. The wind of the Spirit has blown over Job, remaking him, filling him with wisdom, and there in the midst of the storm, he has been turned into a proverb of dust and ashes, and he speaks like a king.

We noted earlier that Job complains of the friends' speeches as "proverbs of ashes" (13:12). This is like what Solomon says about proverbs in the mouths of fools: it's like a "lame man's legs, which hang useless" (Prov. 26:7) or like "a thorn that goes up into the hand of a drunkard" (Prov. 26:9). Not only are the friends useless to Job, but they are ultimately dangerous for the people of Job's kingdom. They are grasping for power and influence, but Job is a wise and faithful king who has suffered patiently for the sake of his people, even for the sake of some of those people who have bought the lies.

Job ends his words with the request to be shown his sin. If he has hidden sexual sin, he would be glad to be found out and reap the consequences, but he insists that he is innocent (31:1–12). If he has despised the cause of the poor or any of his servants, he would be glad to be dismembered, but again he insists that he has always defended the weak and provided for the needy (31:13–23). Likewise, if he has been greedy for gold or secretly rejoiced in his own might and power or rejoiced at the downfall of his enemies, he would welcome the judgment of God (31:24–32). If he has hidden any sin like Adam, he would be glad to have it displayed for him (31:33–34), but what he really wants is an answer. "Oh, that I had one to hear me! (Here is my signature! Let the Almighty answer me!) Oh, that I had the indictment written by my adversary! Surely I would carry it on my shoulder; I would bind it on me as a crown. I would give him an account of all my steps; like a prince I would approach him" (31:35–37).

All of this wrestling and struggle is driving toward what Job really wants: to come face-to-face with God. He wants to wrestle with God until he bestows a blessing upon him, until he becomes a prince of God like Jacob. This pleading, praying, and arguing is the speech of a king, and he is sure that it is the truth, and he is even willing to be cursed with thistles and weeds should he be lying (31:38–39). Job says that if he has done evil and hidden his sin like Adam, let that original curse come upon him (Gen. 3:17–19). What Job says is true; he has been righteous and faithful in the dust. He is speaking like a prince in the dust, and so he pleads for blessing. Proverbs are coming out of his mouth. He is a proverb; a walking, living proverb of God, so he speaks the wisdom of God. And that is where Job's words end (31:40).

Even here in the "ending" of Job's words there is an echo of the prologue in the word "end." The word is *tamu* which is related to the word *tam*, the word for perfect, blameless, or complete. Job finishes speaking, and just as his words were righteous in the prologue, just as he did not sin with his mouth, so too here we are reminded of that faithfulness. His words are completed and perfected. The words of Job are blameless.

## Conclusion

Wisdom and understanding are fundamentally a poetic enterprise. It's a proverbial enterprise. Job's understanding and wisdom are based on being able to see and say what things are like. Like a Solomon who must judge between the words of prostitutes, Job must judge and rule in the midst of a storm, in the midst of fierce argument.

Job has struggled and wrestled through a war of words, and his words have emerged victorious from the battle as proverbs. His words emerge from the battle as kingly wisdom. Job has fought like a king, learning the wisdom of the dust of death. The way to wise rule, true nobility, and royalty is through death. Job has fought like a king, going down into the grave, and he has emerged a king. He has emerged as a prince, crying out for a meeting with God.

This is what happens with the Lord Jesus Christ. He went down into the dust of death, the grave, and the tomb, and he burst out of it. He took the dust of death, and he turned it into a place of new creation. In Jesus, the place of cursing has been turned into a place of blessing. Jesus, in his humility, has turned the curse of the cross into glory and salvation. The slave of all has become the Lord of all. That's the wisdom of the dust of death. The wisdom of the dust of death is that in serving, dying, and losing everything, there is hope and faith that it comes back; that in that death, in that dust there is kingship. There is rule in the dust and glory in the dust. We see this in Job, who is but a dim reflection of Christ.

Gustavo Gutierrez notes that this maturation story in Job is also illustrated through Job's identification with the poor and the needy.[4] As Job recognizes himself in the position of the orphan (6:27) despised and rejected (19:13–19), he becomes an advocate for the weak (26:1–4; 27:13–23; 29:12–17; 31:13–23). From one angle this is like Christ who humbled himself and took the form of a slave. Christ became a slave and died the death of a criminal in order to save his people, who were slaves and criminals. He became the curse in order to free his people *from* the curse. He who knew no sin became sin for us that we might become the righteousness of God in him. What Jesus lives out and effects in his own life, death,

---

4. Gustavo Gutiérrez, *On Job: God-talk and the Suffering of the Innocent*, tr. Matthew J. O'Connell (Maryknoll, NY: Orbis Books, 1987).

and resurrection, he also exhorts his followers to imitate. We see this in Matthew 25 in the parable of the sheep and the goats.

In the parable, Jesus argues that his true sheep are those who find him and serve him in the "least of these my brethren." Those who truly love Christ look for him and serve him through the weak and needy around them. Entering into the suffering of the weak brings individuals *face-to-face* with Christ. Christ says that *he* is the one who is clothed, fed, and befriended. Service, suffering, and struggling for the defense and comfort of the hurting and rejected is fellowship with Jesus, and results in his commendation. As the parable insists, this can be a surprising, unexpected conclusion. The sheep wonder when they served Christ and the goats wonder when they didn't.

Gutierrez says this is a gloss on 1 Corinthians 13, where love of others is a mirror in which we see Christ dimly, and love is the excellent way toward the end of seeing Jesus face-to-face. Loving others, serving them, defending the weak, clothing the naked, and feeding the hungry, as acts of true love and compassion, are steps toward seeing Jesus. In Job, it is his suffering; the accusations and the loss which leads him to argue for justice for himself. As we have seen, this must also include his people—his kingdom. Job's struggle is not merely an individual's temper tantrum. Job's losses are a severe shock to his entire community, and the three satans, the oppressors, are bringing his people down with them. As Job points to the ways of God, implicitly convicting the friends of their own evil intentions, of their plots and treachery, Job becomes the victim, the scapegoat, and the innocent orphan. This identification with death and oppression is the very path which leads Job back into glory and ultimately to encounter Yahweh in the whirlwind. The darkness of death, pain, and accusations is how we see now only "dimly," but this gives way to a conference with Yahweh, face-to-face.

# 9

## CHILDISH WISDOM: JOB 32–37

Have you ever yelled at a character in a television show or a movie? "Don't open that door! Stop being so stupid!" Or maybe you've wanted to stand up and cheer in the middle of the theater at some particularly well-played conversation or heroic action. Elihu is something like that in the book of Job, and in important ways, Elihu represents every reader and hearer of the story. Elihu was not introduced in the beginning of the narrative, and he has said nothing throughout these thirty-one chapters. Elihu is one of many who witnessed these dialogues. Where the speeches were delivered, and whether there was a large crowd gathered around for the entire event or this was an argument that took place over several days, weeks, or months, are all details that are not given. When Job finally rests his case, Elihu cannot bear to let it go without standing up and inserting his thoughts on the matter. He stands up in the middle of the assembly, calls out to the main characters, and offers his opinions.

Elihu shows up out of nowhere to speak. He is briefly introduced by the narrator, and then he monologues, giving four speeches, and then we never hear from him again. When Yahweh evaluates Job and his three friends in the epilogue, Elihu is not even mentioned. He stands up, says his piece, and then disappears. It's almost as if when Elihu stands up the story is paused, and when he finishes, the story continues without any knowledge of Elihu's input. I say "almost" because I believe that Elihu really is an original part to the story, and not a later insertion as many commentators propose.

It is this disconnected interaction with the story that makes Elihu a great representative of every reader and listener of the story. If we have been paying attention, we should have had moments when we wanted to yell at the characters in the story. If we have any sense of justice or concern for Job, we ought to find places where we want to talk back to the speakers.

Elihu also represents us in his ambiguity. What exactly is he saying? If he is saying the same thing the other three friends said, why doesn't Yahweh rebuke *him* at the end? On the other hand, if he's saying something different or fundamentally right, why isn't he commended at the end? Not only are we like Elihu in our responsiveness to the debate up to this point, Elihu is a further invitation into the debate. Some of the more diverse opinions on the book of Job center on the character of Elihu. For most of the medieval and patristic eras, Elihu was viewed with great disdain. On one hand, many considered Elihu to be saying the same thing as the other three friends, and he was labeled and depicted as a demonic figure and even the Satan himself returned as an angel of light.[1] On the other hand, John Calvin viewed Elihu as something like the hero of the story. Susan Schreiner describes Calvin's view of Elihu

---

1. See Lawrence Besserman, *The Legend of Job in the Middle Ages* (Cambridge, MA: Harvard University Press, 1979), 55.

as teaching "undiluted 'Calvinist' doctrine."[2] Calvin sees Elihu as reminding Job that God is truly just and does not act contrary to justice, even though his justice is sometimes partly hidden to human perception in history.[3] Is Elihu the hero, perhaps a John–the–Baptist-like forerunner to Yahweh? Is Elihu the Satan returned in the guise of piety trying one more time to squash Job's integrity? Or is he somewhere in between?

Remember that Job has just emerged as a king in the midst of his trials. God has turned him into a proverb. Job speaks with the wisdom of a king from the dust and the ashes. This nobility and kingliness is not self-righteous pride. It is ultimately faith and hope in the God of the resurrection. We've pointed out several times that for all of Job's negativity, pessimism, and cursing, there are repeated glimpses of what Job is driving at. There is a cunning to his cursing, a reason for the ranting. Perhaps like something not too far removed from David at the gates of Gath, Job is driving at death, daring the friends to strike him down, but he's also driving at what is on the other side of death. "I know that my Redeemer lives," Job cries defiantly. He puts his faith and his hope in the God of the judgment, the God who will judge, the God who raises the dead.

Part of the appeal of Elihu for many is based on a truncated view of the argument between Job and the three friends. If all that is going on is a theological and philosophical argument over the justice of God in the face of evil, then some of Job's raving seems over the top. Elihu can sound a welcome moderating tone to the debate. On the other hand, if Job is quite literally arguing for his life (and winning) then his growing into the wisdom of a king and the cunning of a son of God, is a central motif that grants greater credibility to his ranting and raving. We will walk through Elihu's speeches and then return to the question of his role in the overall story.

---

2. Susan E. Schreiner, "Through a Mirror Dimly: Calvin's Sermons on Job," *Calvin Theological Journal,* 21 (1986), 186.
3. Ibid.

# Childish Wisdom

## Elihu's First Speech (Job 32–33)

The introduction tells us that Elihu is the son of Barachel the Buzite, of the family of Ram (32:2). Elihu is a Hebrew. There is a "Buz" mentioned as descendent of Nahor—Abraham's father in Genesis 22:21—as well as a "Buz" who is descended from Gad much later in history (1 Chron. 5:14). Likewise, there are a few "Rams" scattered through the genealogies, but there is nothing conclusive (Ruth 4:19; 1 Chron. 2:9–27). His name means something like "He is my God." The name is closely related to the name for Elijah: in Hebrew, Elijah is literally *Eliahu*.

We're also told that Elihu is furious (32:2). "Then Elihu the son of Barachel the Buzite, of the family of Ram, *burned with anger*. He *burned with anger* at Job because he justified himself rather than God. He *burned with anger* also at Job's three friends because they had found no answer, although they had declared Job to be in the wrong. Now Elihu had waited to speak to Job because they were older than he. And when Elihu saw that there was no answer in the mouth of these three men, he *burned with anger*" (32:2–4, emphasis added).

Elihu's wrath is mentioned four times. In Hebrew, to be angry is to burn. Elihu is furious. His wrath is aroused in a fourfold way against Job and the three friends. Literally, it says that he thinks that Job has justified himself rather than God or more than God (32:1–2). Elihu is angry because Job thinks he's more just and more righteous than God.

Elihu is also angry that the three friends have not been able to answer Job (32:3). Though they have tried, they have not been able to answer him. He burned with anger when he saw that "there was no answer in the mouth of the three men." Perhaps Elihu is upset with the content of their answers, but this doesn't seem likely given what he ends up saying. Elihu is mad that they have become silent. There are no more words/answers in their mouths. Elihu is angry because they have allowed Job to take the microphone unchallenged.

When Elihu begins, the narrator helps him a bit by offering an explanation. Elihu is a young guy, and he realizes that it's not his place to jump into the middle of a conversation (32:4). He knows age and wisdom go first, and he has been waiting for an appropriate opportunity to speak. He says he'll speak now, since they're all done talking (32:5).

It all sounds humble at first, but Elihu keeps going. "Therefore I say, 'Listen to me; let me also declare my opinion.' . . . Behold, I waited for your words, I listened for your wise sayings, while you searched out what to say" (32:10–11). This sort of preparatory monologing goes on and on, and he keeps coming back to it. Later Elihu says, "But now, hear my speech, O Job, and listen to all my words. Behold, I open my mouth; the tongue in my mouth speaks. My words declare the uprightness of my heart, and what my lips know they speak sincerely" (33:1–3). Then again he says, "Hear my words, you wise men, and give ear to me, you who know; for the ear tests words as the palate tastes food" (34:2–3). He begins his final speech the same way: "Bear with me a little, and I will show you, for I have yet something to say on God's behalf. I will get my knowledge from afar and ascribe righteousness to my Maker. For truly my words are not false; one who is perfect in knowledge is with you" (36:2–4).

Elihu is full of words; in fact, that's exactly what he says: "I am full of words, the Spirit within me" (32:18). The word for spirit here is "wind." Elihu is full of windy words. He says that this wind is within him, in his belly, like wine that has no vent. It's ready to burst like new wineskins (32:18–19). The word in 32:19 for "belly" can also be used for "womb." The word for "burst" is sometimes used in a violent way to refer to wombs that are struck open in warfare. Elihu is using very strange language here; it seems extreme, over the top, even melodramatic. Elihu *almost* sounds like he is describing himself as a windbag and a drunkard. Of course, Elihu doesn't mean that, but the whole story of Job leads up to this. We've seen this imagery before; Job and his friends used it as an insult toward one another earlier. Job says that his friends are just blowing wind (6:26, 16:3, 30:15), and Eliphaz and Bildad have said the same of Job's words (8:2, 15:2). Elihu says it of himself—"Hey guys, I'm full of wind too!"

Elihu goes on to say that he is the answer to Job's request; he is Job's mouth before God. "Behold, I open my mouth; the tongue in my mouth speaks. My words declare the uprightness of my heart, and what my lips know they speak sincerely. The Spirit of God has made me, and the breath of the Almighty gives me life. Answer me, if you can; set your words in order before me; take your stand. Behold, I am toward God as you are" (33:2–6). Literally, "I am toward God as you are" is "I am as your mouth to God." Elihu claims that he is going to play the part of arbiter and mediator, speaking on God's behalf as well as Job's.

What does Elihu say on behalf of God? He says that Job is not right to insist that he is innocent (33:12). Job should stop asking for an answer because God doesn't give answers (33:13). Actually, God does give answers, but not like Job is looking for. Sometimes God speaks in one way or another. Sometimes he speaks in a dream or a vision (33:15). He opens men's ears and tries to give them instruction. He does this to protect them, to prevent them from falling into pits or perishing by the sword (33:16–22). He sometimes also sends messengers and mediators—literally, "an interpreter"—"to declare to man what is right for him" (33:23). Elihu implies that this is what *he* is doing. Elihu says that he is God's messenger sent to save Job, to protect him.

Elihu says something we have heard before, but he does bring in a bit more of the context. He understands what Job is after; Job wants a meeting with God, to speak with him. Elihu says that this is impossible and God isn't available like this. God sends dreams, visions, and messengers, and these are inspired by God and should suffice for Job. In other words, Elihu is referring to the "vision" that Eliphaz saw (4:12–21), the words of the three friends, as well as Elihu himself. Job should stop crying out to meet with God because God has sent messengers! Elihu says that he and the other three friends are the word of God to Job. God gives two or three chances to a man to listen to him, Elihu says, in order to "bring back his soul from the pit" (33:29–30). He says that Job is going on four chances, and he really must listen.

Elihu concludes his first speech with these words: "Pay attention, O Job, listen to me; be silent, and I will speak. If you have any words, answer me; speak, for I desire to justify you. If not, listen to me; be silent, and I will teach you wisdom" (33:31–33), and then immediately jumps into his second speech: "Hear my words" (34:1–2).

### ELIHU'S SECOND SPEECH (JOB 34)

In Elihu's second speech, he says that it isn't fitting for a wicked king to act as a judge (34:17). Elihu understands the political tension better than the other three friends. Job, remember, is a king. He is a ruler over many, and the kingdom is in jeopardy. The "friends" are most likely counselors or nobility from the land. Job's whole nation is at stake, so Elihu ties his second speech directly to kings. He says that people do not just go up to kings and correct them (34:18). On the other hand, God is not partial to men in authority either. God can speak to those people and correct them, and he does not regard the rich more than the poor. They are all the work of his hands (34:19). Therefore, Elihu says that it is God's place to rebuke kings and nobles. He does this providentially, when bad things happen to them, when calamities strike suddenly (34:20). His eyes are open on all the ways of man (34:21). God sees all his steps; there is no darkness or shadow of death where the workers of iniquity may hide themselves, whether a king or a pauper (34:22–29). God personally makes sure that hypocrites do not reign to lead astray the people (34:30).

Job has been accused of blasphemy, and Elihu has heard wise men urging a full trial and conviction (34:34–37). The subtext to this speech is that Job doesn't need a trial. Elihu says that God sees everything; what's happening now to Job *is* his judgment. God breaks in pieces mighty men without inquiry (34:24). God does not need a subpoena. God does not need to get a warrant for an arrest. God knows it all and he acts righteously. Not anybody can confront a king, but *God* can, and God confronts kings by throwing them down. Job has been thrown down, Elihu says, so let's do the math. Elihu finally comes out in the clear here, though he has tried to hold a neutral tone. Here, he agrees that Job's words and situation imply his wickedness.

### ELIHU'S THIRD SPEECH (JOB 35)

In Elihu's third speech, he again answers himself and asks, "Do you think this to be just? Do you say, 'It is my right before God,' that you ask, 'What advantage have I? How am I better off than if I had sinned?' I will answer you and your friends with you" (35:2–4). Elihu says that Job is implying that he is more righteous than God, because he says that it doesn't matter if he's righteous or not. God sometimes strikes good people and blesses evil people. In other words, Elihu says that Job thinks he is more righteous than God, because he has some basis on which he can appeal to God. That must mean Job believes God is unrighteous in some way, because Job thinks he can appeal to God and get hearing.

Elihu again insists that *he* is the answer from God (35:4), but more importantly, God doesn't need to answer Job. Nothing we do, righteous or wicked, really affects God (35:5–8). Is God challenged? Is God hurt? Can we add anything to him? Can we take anything away from him? God is under no obligation to answer prideful men (35:9–13). The fact that he does not answer does not impugn his justice, it only confirms Job's ignorance (35:14–16). Elihu says that this is evident from the heavens and the clouds and even in the animal kingdom.

### ELIHU'S FOURTH SPEECH (JOB 36–37)

Elihu's fourth and final speech returns to the claim that he speaks on behalf of God. "Bear with me a little, and I will show you, for I have yet something to say on God's behalf. I will get my knowledge from afar and ascribe righteousness to my Maker. For truly my words are not false; one who is perfect in knowledge is with you" (36:2–4). Elihu claims that his knowledge is from God, and it is "perfect" and "blameless"; yet Elihu repeats what the other friends have argued. He tells Job to confess his sin, and everything will be restored. Like in his second speech, Elihu applies his principles of justice and God's goodness specifically to kings. God is mighty, omnipotent., and just. The righteous are on thrones with kings (36:5–7). He has seated them forever, and they are exalted. If kings are brought down, it's because they were wicked (36:8–15). Job is a king, and he was brought down. The fact that God has not answered Job's prayers for restoration to this point indicates Job's wickedness even further (36:16–21).

Elihu claims that when affliction falls upon a king, it proves that God's favor is not with him. Elihu reminds Job that God is great and mighty. He is the great teacher (36:22), and therefore who can suggest that God has done wrong (36:23)? The final paragraphs of Elihu's fourth speech illustrate God's greatness with the image of a terrific thunderstorm.

> Behold, God is great, and we know him not; the number of his years is unsearchable. For he draws up the drops of water; they distill his mist in rain, which the skies pour down and drop on mankind abundantly. Can anyone understand the spreading of the clouds, the thunderings of his pavilion? Behold, he scatters his lightning about him and covers the roots of the sea. For by these he judges peoples; he gives food in abundance. He covers his hands with the lightning and commands it to strike the mark. Its crashing declares his presence; the cattle also declare that he rises. At this also my heart trembles and leaps out of its place. Keep listening to the thunder of his voice and the rumbling that comes from his mouth. Under the whole heaven he lets it go, and his lightning to the corners of the earth. After it his voice roars; he thunders with his majestic voice, and he does not restrain the lightnings when his voice is heard. God thunders wondrously with his voice; he does great things that we cannot comprehend. For to the snow he says, "Fall on the earth," likewise to the downpour, his mighty downpour. He seals up the hand of every man, that all men whom he made may know it. Then the beasts go into their lairs, and remain in their dens. From its chamber comes the whirlwind, and cold from the scattering winds. By the breath of God ice is given, and the broad waters are frozen fast. He loads the thick cloud with moisture; the clouds scatter his lightning. They turn around and around by his guidance, to ac-

complish all that he commands them on the face of the habitable world. Whether for correction or for his land or for love, he causes it to happen. (36:26–37:13)

Elihu says that God is a storm. God speaks in the storm; he echoes his voice in thunder and lightning, rain and snow, ice and wind. "Hear this, O Job; stop and consider the wondrous works of God. Do you know how God lays his command upon them and causes the lightning of his cloud to shine? Do you know the balancings of the clouds, the wondrous works of him who is perfect in knowledge, you whose garments are hot when the earth is still because of the south wind? Can you, like him, spread out the skies, hard as a cast metal mirror? Teach us what we shall say to him" (37:14–19). What do we say to this storm, Job? "We cannot draw up our case because of darkness. Shall it be told him that I would speak?" (37:19). Do you talk to a storm, Job, and ask for a meeting? "Did a man ever wish that he would be swallowed up? And now no one looks on the light when it is bright in the skies, when the wind has passed and cleared them. Out of the north comes golden splendor; God is clothed with awesome majesty. The Almighty—we cannot find him" (37:20–23). Elihu says that God is a mighty storm. He beats upon us. He is great; he is all-powerful, and Elihu insists that he is good: "He is great in power; justice and abundant righteousness he will not violate. Therefore men fear him; he does not regard any who are wise in their own conceit" (37:23–24). Because God is such a great and terrible storm, Elihu tells Job to stop expecting God to speak with him. Instead, Job needs to submit to the storm and repent of his sin. That is all anyone can do.

Then 38:1: "Then the Lord answered Job out of the whirlwind." Elihu is wrong. The whirlwind speaks. The storm speaks. The God of lightning and thunder, rain, snow and ice; the God of the wind, the God of all these terrors, *answers Job*. Job serves the God who *answers*.

The three friends stopped answering Job because he was righteous in his own eyes, but Elihu burns with anger, continuing their storm of words. He is given four consecutive speeches, the wind of his words blowing harder and harder. Of course, he claims to be the wind of God, and in a sense, he is. He is the storm, growing closer and closer. When he thinks he's the end of the storm, God steps in to take over and answers Job.

Another way to trace the themes of the prologue through the arguments of the middle of the book is by following the *words*. Matthew Lynch notes that the "damage" done to Job only begins in the prologue, and the calamity continues in the form of the verbal onslaught of Job's friends. Lynch points out specifically that "from the beginning, Job is assailed by words, by the breathless reports of his three servants, the biting words of his wife, and by his three companions." Lynch points out the repetition of the phrase "while he was still speaking, another came and said" in chapter 1.[4]

In this sense, the trials of Job always come in the form of words. From the beginning, Job is pummeled with words. Before one speaker has finished, another arrives with more bad news. On the surface, it is interesting that there are four speeches in the prologue announcing each calamity, and there are four speakers who declare to Job their opinions regarding his complaint. Quite possibly there is another layer in the simple fact that Elihu gives four speeches as well. He piles on, and his windy words are the equivalent of all four messengers in the first chapter.

Lynch also points out that Elihu in particular highlights the "out of nowhere" character of these word-attacks.[5] The initial calamities in chapter 1 are clearly out of nowhere; Job was not expecting them. Similarly, after the words of Job are ended in 31:40, it would read quite naturally to run right into Yahweh's response, but Elihu bursts on the scene with his many words. It is also noteworthy that Yahweh never acknowledges Elihu. At the very least, this highlights Elihu's speeches as apparently random — out of nowhere — and in this sense very similar to the initial reports from the messenger and servants. Elihu and his friends are *more* calamity;

---

4. Matthew Lynch, "Bursting at the Seams: Phonetic Rhetoric in the Speeches of Elihu," *Journal for the Study of Old Testament* 30.3 (2006), 348.

5. Ibid., 349.

they continue the storm with their accusations and denunciations. Elihu is the culmination of the calamities and words of the accuser that blow against Job.[6]

Another indication that the speeches of Elihu are not a substantial advance in the argument is how the narrator introduces two of Elihu's speeches with the words "Elihu answered and said" (34:1; 35:1). This phrase could be read as referring more generally to the entire conversation, but unlike the rest of the speeches and answers between Job and the three friends, Elihu has no immediate discussion partner. No one answers Elihu. He is not really answering anyone except himself. William Henry Green suggests Job doesn't respond to Elihu because Job is convinced of what Elihu says.[7] Likewise, Green says that Yahweh doesn't answer Elihu directly because Elihu was offering a "verdict" to the legal battle that has played out, and Yahweh substantially agrees with Elihu and views his judgment as "preliminary to his own."[8] Green says it would not really do for Yahweh to answer a human creature or enter into argument with him as though his justice might be scrutinized by human judgment. However, this is the very same claim that Elihu and the three friends have repeatedly made. In order to defend Elihu, Green and others must resort to arguing Elihu's central point.

## Conclusion

If the book of Job is in part the record of one man growing up from immaturity to maturity, going from the glory of a priest to the glory of a prophet, going from outside the assembly of the sons of God to being ushered into the whirlwind presence of God, perhaps this gives us a few clues about the role Elihu as the youthful counselor at the end of the debates.

---

6. These several paragraphs drawing from Matthew Lynch are taken substantially from my essay in *The Glory of Kings: A Festschrift for James B. Jordan*.

7. William Henry Green, *Conflict and Triumph: The Argument of the Book of Job Unfolded* (Carlisle, PA: Banner of Truth Trust, 1999), 125.

8. Ibid., 125–26.

First, as we have noted, there are good reasons to see Elihu as foolish. His own rhetorical style is over the top and quite simply humorous. Some commentators suggest that Elihu was originally intended as the "court jester" or comedic intermission. Whether that is true or not, there are unmistakable oddities about Elihu's speeches that stretch his credibility. One way we can account for this is the fact that Elihu is young (32:4, 6), and perhaps this explains why he is not explicitly condemned by God in the end. Yahweh doesn't condemn Elihu for his foolishness because of his youth. Elihu is young and probably not a high ranking official in the kingdom like the other three friends. In short, he is not a political threat to Job like the three court advisers are. Or more directly, Elihu isn't trying to maneuver Job off the throne and have him executed. He is an innocent spectator. As we have said, he represents us, the readers. Elihu has been biting his lip over the course of the dialogues, and he has now jumped in to give his two, three, or four cents. He appears to repeat the main arguments of the three friends (with some improvements), but he isn't repeating the arguments in a *deceitful* way. He honestly believes that Job needs to be corrected. Elihu is young and given his gusto, we should see his folly as the folly of youth. He is immature.

This suggests a reading of Job that focuses on generational themes and tensions. For instance, the three "older" advisers are "younger" in stature, since they are apparently nobles or lesser magistrates of some sort. Job is the "older" king in so far as he is their political superior, but in another sense, Job is still "young" in so far as he is contrasted at the beginning of the book with the "sons of God." The sons of God who assemble before the face of Yahweh are "older" than Job; they have been granted even greater glory and greater authority as advisers to the King of Kings. The dialogues also suggest that Job is literally younger than the three counselors (15:10). In this sense, the dialogues of Job set up a situation vaguely parallel to that of Rehoboam in 1 Kings 12, only here, instead of the older sages giving sound advice, they are counseling folly and the younger "advisor" is not much better.

Even though Elihu is an immature fool, he nevertheless signifies something true about what Job must become. Elihu is a foolish, ignorant child, but Job must also become a child. We have noted how Job's wisdom emerges through suffering and death as Christ clearly teaches and embodies in the gospel, but Christ also teaches that his wisdom calls his disciples to become like little children (Matt. 19:14; Mark 10:15). He who is least will be the greatest (Luke 9:47–48). In order for Job to grow up into maturity and greatness, he must become young. Thus, Elihu is the transition from Job's "old," foolish counselors to the youthfulness of the Lord of the whirlwind, the King who plays with dragons (41:5). Elihu is wrong and foolish like the others, but he is a lesser fool in so far as he is a young fool. Elihu is the wrong sort of child, but, like every child, he points to the truth. We must be young again. Unless we are born again, we will not see the kingdom of God. The story of Job is thus an extended narrative of one man's being born again. We noted at the beginning that Job tearing his clothes and falling to the ground in worship was reminiscent of Adam in the garden, and his own words suggest a "re-birth" theme when he says that he came from his mother's womb naked and he will return there naked (1:20–21).

This reading also suggests a helpful way of looking at the genres employed in the narrative of Job. As we noted at the beginning of the story, the prologue opens like a fairy tale. Carol Newsom calls it a "didactic tale," drawing off of elements of fairy tale as well as prophetic or parabolic tales.[9] She interacts with Susan Suleiman's work *Authoritarian Fiction*, who notes that didactic literature "infantilizes the reader." Newsom explains, "The subject position that didactic narratives offer the reader of whatever age is that of a child." In other words, fairy tales are not only for children, fairytales (or "didactic tales") have a way of *creating* children. The genre of fairy tale, parable, or didactic tale as Newsom calls it, revels in security and reassurance, a simple and unified vision of the world and morality, and all from an authoritative voice. In order to

---

9. Carol A. Newsom, *The Book of Job: A Contest of Moral Imaginations* (Oxford: Oxford University Press, 2003).

enter the world of the fairy tale, listeners must enter the imaginative world of a childlike consciousness and faith. Jesus clearly plays with some of these expectations in his parables: not only is he calling his disciples to become like children and to receive little children, he trains them and disciples them in the ways of the child-kingdom by telling them parables. In other words, the genre of Jesus' stories assumes—and even creates—a child audience. If parables have, at least on the surface, a "paternal" voice, then Jesus is the Word of the Father for the children of Israel. We can also say that the parables are children's stories only appreciated and loved by those who have "become children" for the Kingdom. Those who "have ears to hear" are children. These stories of Jesus are one of the effective ways that Jesus calls into being and creates a childish people. Listening to the stories of Jesus in faith is the way to become children who may enter the Kingdom. Parables are stories that create children.

In this sense, the genre structure of the book of Job may make more sense. Commentators puzzle over why the story of Job is framed with the didactic, fairy tale prose. It's sort of cute, perhaps, to end with a nice-sounding story, but are the prologue and epilogue merely the "husk" of the story that the author hijacked for the real point, that is, the dialogues? This doesn't seem right. If the story of Job is the story of a great king growing up into greater glory, then the story is all about a wise king growing up into the wisdom of a child. The success of that educational process, the success of the story, would then be clearly evident in the return to the fairy tale genre. The king must emerge as greater and wiser in the epilogue, but in some ways, we hope and expect to see him more childlike.

In this sense, Elihu seems to be perfectly placed and fitted for this story. There is no need to demonize him completely, even if he does still echo the Accuser in certain respects. His "windy words" can still function as transition from the older men (who should have been wise) to God, who is the "oldest" since he was there when the foundations of the earth were laid (38:4). Elihu is certainly right to see God in the storm, even if he did not think Job was right to request a meeting with the Storm. Elihu's childish folly gives way to the whirling and spinning songs of Yahweh, which take the childishness to a whole new level. They reveal in a spectacular fashion the childlike giddiness and joy which Job is growing up into.

This childlike wisdom points to childlike faith, and Job is a great example of faith. Despite what the accusers say, despite what the words say, despite what the messengers say—all of them—Job says, "As long as my breath is in me, as long as the breath of God is in my nostrils, my lips will not speak wickedness, nor my tongue utter deceit. Far be it from me that I should say you are right. Till I die, I will not put away my integrity from me. My righteousness I hold fast and will not let it go. My heart shall not reproach me as long as I live" (27:4–6). This is the faith of Job, and we have noted how this faith has been perceived as folly by the friends. They think he is crazy, scandalous, and stubbornly foolish, but Job has been growing up into the wisdom of a child. The dialogues have been a tutorial, an educational program in childish wisdom.

This challenges Christians to childlike faith in Christ. Do you cling to your integrity like Job? Do you speak and pray like him? Job does not claim to be sinless; Job claims to be perfect. We are no different. We are not sinless, but we are righteous. We are not sinless, but we are perfect in Christ. Paul says that we are to reckon ourselves dead to sin and alive to God in Christ; therefore, we are to disobey sin.

Job knows he is not sinless, but he also knows that he has been faithful. Fundamentally, he *loves* God, and because he loves God, he wants to talk to him face-to-face. This is the audacity of childlike faith. Elihu is in some ways like the disciples, insisting that God cannot be bothered with blessing the little children, but Yahweh answers out of the storm and calls to his beloved son Job. Yahweh says, "Let the little children come to me." He would be glad to speak to Job, for of such is the kingdom of God.

# 10

## THE STORM SPEAKS: JOB 38–42

If there has been high Hebrew poetry to this point in the book of Job, it all pales in comparison to the answers of Yahweh. This section, where God himself speaks to Job, is one of the most glorious passages in all of Scripture. Here God celebrates creation, all the details, all the care he gives to the world, all of these nooks and crannies where his glory is revealed—down to the depths of the sea, in the night, in the day, in wind, in stars, and even the animals. All of creation is marvelous, glorious, and wonderfully reflects the glory and wisdom of its Maker.

Then we step back and remember: this is God *talking*. Not only is creation amazing and glorious, but God celebrates it, all excited about what he made. "Look at this," he keeps saying, "and this! I made that! Isn't it wonderful?" If Job is a new creation story, the story of God remaking a man and his world, then this is the end of the day where he sees all that he has made and says that it's all very good. This is the Sabbath of the creation week, and by his mere delight, God blesses all that he has made.

*What* God is saying is glorious, the fact that God is the one *saying it* is glorious, and then even more so, we have to remember that he is saying it all to Job! On one level this is amazing and mindblowing simply because God is talking to a man. Job was a man with ten fingers and ten toes, a belly button, and a nose. The God who made that pile of dust appears to Job and begins dancing, shouting, and looking at everything he has made: "Do you see this?" "Have you seen the ostrich?" God is excited, and if we are reading carefully we can feel it.

Throughout the book of Job, Job's steadfast hope has been in the God who judges and speaks. Over and over again, Job says that he wants to hear from God himself. He wants to have a meeting with God. The friends tell him he's crazy; he can't speak to God, but Job keeps crying out for a meeting with God, and Elihu enters the scene and tells him one last time that what he's asking for is impossible. God speaks through prophets, through visions, through angels, but God is a terrible storm and Job can't talk to the storm. God is just too big, too out of control, too righteous.

Yet in 38:1, that terrible and righteous storm—God himself— answers Job. God vindicates Job, right in front of Elihu, and they have their meeting.

Of course, God is far more glorious and wonderful than even Job can hope for. In many ways, Job has been insisting upon the glory of God, and Job's hope is that even that glory can extend to something so mundane as a meeting with him. But insisting that Mt. Everest is amazing, mindboggling, stupendous, fantastic, and awful is nothing compared to actually climbing it. The horror of actually finding yourself on the side of the mountain, as I'm sure many climbers have felt, is far worse (and more wonderful) than they could have imagined even after months or years of training.

Remember that Job is an Adam. Back in chapter 1, Job was a man in a beautiful garden, surrounded by animals that he cared for and tended. He had dominion over the earth. He had a wife and children. He had been fruitful and multiplied, and he worshipped God faithfully. God was pleased with him, and he was perfect. Job was an Adam.

Then, right on schedule, Satan showed up in the garden. Shortly after, Job's world was unmade, messenger by messenger. Job's initial curse, after he sat in silence for seven days in ashes and mourning, continued the process. He said, "Let there be darkness"—not "let there be light," not "let the world spring out of nothing"—but "let it all go back to nothing. Let there be darkness." Job also says, "Let the night go back. May darkness seize the day." At creation, light and darkness were separated, creating day and night, but Job wanted it all to go back to darkness and chaos.

In Job's initial curse, he said, "May those who curse it curse the day, those who are ready to arouse Leviathan" (3:8). There in his misery, he cries out for the biggest monster he can think of to unmake the world. "Call for the dragon, and may he come and unmake the world, destroy the world, decreate it all, make it all go away." Remember that Job's longing for death and darkness is ultimately related to his longing for a day of judgment, a day when he might appeal his case to God. If the world is unmade, the only thing left is God.

Not only does all this death and darkness move Job into the presence of God through de-creation, but also through sacrifice. Remember the beginning of the book, where Job offered sacrifices for his sons. Through those Ascension Offerings, Job symbolically sent his sons into the presence of God. As the smoke ascended, so did his sons. Yahweh has been doing something similar with his beloved son Job. He is a faithful father and his plan has been at work all along, drawing Job up into his presence. Job is perfect, blameless, without spot or wrinkle, just like a sacrificial animal. God draws Job into a fiery storm, so Job can ascend to his presence.

We've traced that storm. It begins with the wind and fire falling on Job, but that isn't the end. The wind increases in the storm of words from Job's friends. It increases even more with Elihu, and finally, Job finds himself in the whirlwind of God's presence. Think of the thunder cloud that led Israel out of Egypt and through the wilderness. Think of the electrical storm that descended on Mt. Sinai. Think of the smoke and thunder when Isaiah saw the Lord high and lifted up. Think of the cloud full of raging fire coming out of the north toward Ezekiel at the River Chebar. Think of Elijah and the fiery chariots and the whirlwind. Job has been drawn up into that fire storm presence, and now he's talking to Yahweh, Lord of heaven and earth.

### YAHWEH'S FIRST SPEECH (JOB 38–39)

Yahweh begins with a question. "Who is this that darkens counsel by words without knowledge?" (38:2). Given the fact that this question comes right on the heels of Elihu's insistence that Job cannot speak to the storm, some have suggested that Yahweh's question is directed at Elihu. Is Elihu the one darkening counsel and speaking without knowledge? However, this interpretation represents a minority, given the fact that the narrator says that Yahweh "answered Job" (38:1), and Job takes Yahweh to be speaking to him (42:3). At the same time, if Yahweh is saying that Job has "darkened counsel" and shown "ignorance," it must be understood in such a way as to be consistent with Yahweh's final commendation of Job "who has spoken what is right" (42:7–8).

Yahweh immediately commands Job to "dress for action like a man" (38:3). This is the language of military preparation (1 Sam. 2:4; 2 Sam. 22:40; Ps. 18:33, 40; Is. 8:9; cf. Job 30:18). Yahweh calls Job to strap on his sword, gird up his loins, and get ready for a tussle. Like we have seen previously, this wrestling match is going to take place with words. God says, "I will question you, and you will make it known to me." This may not be so much a challenge as a promise. Like most good teachers, God is going to ask questions, make observations, and then talk to his student about them. In other words, God is going to *teach* Job, so that he can make it known to him. God is a father, teaching Job, his son. The language of learning and education is full of love and beauty. These questions are not angrily yelled at Job. Yahweh is not a short-tempered, egotistical Father. These are musical words, songs and poetry celebrating and exploring the created universe of seas and stars, rain and light, beasts and birds, and culminating with the behemoth and Leviathan. These are songs and stories about some of God's favorite things in the world, and these songs and stories are invitations for Job, his son, to join in the fun.

God begins by recounting creation: "Where were you when I laid the foundations of the earth? Tell me, if you have understanding. Who determined its measurements? Surely you know. Who stretched the line upon it, to what were its foundations fastened, who laid its cornerstone when the morning stars all sang together and the sons of God shouted for joy?" (38:4–7).

Notice that in the very first poem, in the very first reference to all the things God has done, he refers to the "sons of God." Recall that the sons of God are those men and angels referred to back in 1:6 and 2:1, those who stand before God, who are in his presence when the Accuser comes in. The great tension in the prologue is that Job is the greatest of the sons of the east, but he is not among the sons of God in the presence of God.

The "sons of God" in 38:7 are clearly angels and were in God's presence when the morning stars sang together at the beginning of creation. They were there when the foundations of the earth were laid. They shouted for joy; they cheered God on when he made the world. They know something of what God is talking about. They are the witnesses that he calls.

Notice all the verbs flooding the poems: determine, shut, command, divide, hunt, number. This is all about dominion, rule, and kingship. The creation scenes—vignettes of wild animals—all draw a picture of a world in need of care, taming, ruling, and cultivating. Can Job, another Adam, do that? Can you divide? Can you count? Can you rule? Can you hunt? Can you command and rule? All of this is a wide ranging summary of the wisdom of God in creation, and the concluding question is, "Does the hawk fly by your wisdom?" (39:26).

Yahweh pauses here and addresses Job directly, asking him if he would like to cross-examine him. He asks, "Do you want to keep contending with me? Do you want to continue your case, Job?" (40:2). Job says that he is really of very little account. Some translations say, "Behold, I am vile." Job uses very strong language; he says that he is very little, very small, very insignificant. He is too frail to talk to God; he's like the pinky finger.

This is exactly what Job said he would do: "Even if I stood before God and started talking, I would be driven to silence. I would be dumbfounded. I would be completely blown away, and I would have nothing to say" (9:3, 14–16). Job has nothing to say, so Yahweh proceeds and tells Job to prepare for battle again: "Gird up your loins." God tells Job to prepare for battle, to prepare himself like a man.

### YAHWEH'S SECOND SPEECH (JOB 40–41)

This time, God addresses Job directly. He asks him some very plain questions. "Is Job trying to thwart Yahweh's judgment? Are you trying to cause my judgment to go away?" God asks. "Are you accusing me of evil, that you might be righteous?" (40:8). He asks, "Do you have an arm like God?" He says, if you have an arm like God, let's see it. Flex it. "Can you thunder with a voice like me, adorn yourself with majesty and splendor, array yourself with glory and beauty? Disperse the rage of your wrath, look on everyone who is proud and humble him, look on everyone who is proud and bring him low? Shred down the wicked in their place, hide them in the dust together, bind their faces in hidden darkness. Then I will also confess to you that your own right hand can save you, that you have a mighty arm like God, too" (40:9–14).

These are hard questions and we don't want to downplay them, but we also don't want to play them so loudly that we miss the context. The context here is of God the Father of Job, teaching his son, drawing him into his presence, calling him to follow. Of course, Job is not sinless. It's not as if he has never made any missteps along the way. We know that Job "did not sin with his lips"; however, he is perfect in that regard, and at the end of the book,

God says to Job's friends, "You did not speak what is right as my servant Job has."

Part of the context is recognizing that Job seems to know already most of what Yahweh says. In fact, he actually said some of it before. Job previously insisted that he would not be able to stand before God and he would be speechless if he did (9:2ff), but he also said that he knows God is wise in heart and mighty in strength. Who has hardened himself against him and prospered? "He removes the mountains and they do not know when he overturns them in his anger. He shakes the earth out of its place and its pillars tremble, he commands the sun and it does not rise. He seals off the stars. He alone spreads out the heavens, he treads on the waves of the sea. He made the Bear, Orion, the Pleiades, and the chambers of the south, he does great things past finding out, wonders without number, and if he goes by me, I don't see him; if he moves past, I do not perceive him, and if he takes away, who can hinder him? Who can say to him, what are you doing?" (9:4–9).

So many of the things God points out, Job knows. He knows that God controls all these things; the wind and the stars obey him. He knows that God searches the depths, and that God knows wonders untold.

God is not giving Job new information. Job has never suggested that the world is a simple place or that God is not in control of it. At the same time, surely God at least identifies himself as the great Creator God. God is beyond us in majesty, power, glory, and wisdom, and that is certainly part of what God is saying. Yet there is more going on than just that, and that comes out particularly in God's description of the behemoth and Leviathan.

God says, "Look at the behemoth, which I made along with you, Job. He eats grass like an ox. See how his strength is in his hips, his power is in his stomach muscles. He moves his tail like a cedar. The sinews of his thighs are tightly knit. His bones are like beams of bronze, his ribs like bars of iron. He is first in the ways of God, and only he who made him can bring near his sword" (40:15–19). The behemoth is this mighty creature, this mighty monster, and God says that only he can hunt him.

## The Storm Speaks

Later, describing Leviathan, God asks these questions:

> Can you draw out Leviathan with a fishhook or press down his tongue with a cord? Can you put a rope in his nose or pierce his jaw with a hook? Will he make many pleas to you? Will he speak to you soft words? Will he make a covenant with you to take him for your servant forever? Will you play with him as with a bird, or will you put him on a leash for your girls? Will traders bargain over him? Will they divide him up among the merchants? Can you fill his skin with harpoons or his head with fishing spears? Lay your hands on him; remember the battle—you will not do it again! Behold, the hope of a man is false; he is laid low even at the sight of him. No one is so fierce that he dares to stir him up. Who then is he who can stand before me?" (41:1–10)

The point of these questions is the final one: "Who then is he who can stand before me?" The answer is not "no one." We know it is not "no one" because the "sons of God" *stand* before God—it's the same word. There is a day in which the sons of God come and *stand* before God (1:6, 2:1). They station themselves before Yahweh. and watch him do all these amazing and wild things. They rejoice in him. They shout for joy, rejoicing at God's mighty works (38:7).

There is a great contrast here. God tells Job he is God; perfect, holy, majestic, and awesome. He can do all these things and Job cannot. In so far as Job cannot do all these things, Job cannot stand before God. Job cannot keep up with God. If running the universe were a race, God would beat Job every time.

Then is that really all that God is doing? Is the Lord merely flexing his divine muscles? Is he just telling Job to stop complaining about being human? Many commentators conclude that the primary aim of Yahweh's speeches is to establish his sovereignty. Yahweh does all these things with wisdom, power, and goodness, therefore, Job needs to calm down, stop complaining, and trust God. This means that Yahweh's answer is essentially a rejection of Job's pleas for understanding, for a hearing, for a meeting face-to-face. As Keil and Delitzsch explain, Yahweh "does not exactly do what Job wished . . . he surprises him with questions which are intended to bring him indirectly to the consciousness of the wrong and absurdity of his challenge."[1] Yahweh's answer is an extended survey of his rule over the natural world which is intended to produce humility in Job: "Job knows even before God speaks, and yet he must now hear it, because he does not know it rightly; for the nature with which he is acquainted as the herald of the creative and governing power of God is also the preacher of humility; and exalted as God the Creator and Ruler of the natural world is above Job's censure."[2]

"Since Job cannot answer a single one of those questions taken from the natural kingdom, but, on the contrary, must everywhere admire and adore the power and wisdom of God—he must appear as an insignificant fool, if he applies them to his limited judgment concerning the Author of his affliction."[3]

There are a number of difficulties with this reading, however. First, it misunderstands what God is up to by not giving the prologue sufficient weight. Yahweh is a faithful Father who has used the evil intentions of the Accuser as an opportunity to "sanctify" his son Job through suffering. Yahweh's response cannot be read as though God has been wholly absent and is only now coming down to see what is going on. Rather, Yahweh answers as a faithful Father, rightly challenging his son Job, but he is not merely putting Job "back in his place." Yahweh does not want Job to stay where he is. As we have seen repeatedly, the entire book up to this point has been thrusting Job forward. Job has been struck and he has suffered, but he is being made perfect through suffering. He is going from perfect to perfected. He is being drawn up into the Spirit-wind presence of his Father. The whirlwind answer is first of all an *answer*. It is Job speaking with the Lord of the universe. Job has moved from being a great son in the east who was not among the "sons of God" to becoming a son who stands before his Maker and Father and talks with him.

---

1. F. Delitzsch, *Job, Commentary on the Old Testament in Ten Volumes*, ed. C.F. Keil and F. Delitzsch, tr. Francis Bolton (Grand Rapids, MI: Eerdmans, 1980), 2:312.
2. Ibid., 2:352.
3. Ibid., 2:353.

There are also broader difficulties with this standard line of interpretation offered by Delitzsch. While it is of course absolutely and essentially true that God's power, wisdom, and goodness are on display and are rightly admired and praised, it is *not* the case that Job "cannot answer a single one of those questions." Plainly, certain of them—but not all—are beyond Job's reach. Job could hunt prey for lions and learn about the birthing habits of the mountain goats and the deer. The wild ox may be a very wild and tenacious sort of beast, but Job could probably learn a great deal about its habits and perhaps bring it under his rule. At one point, Yahweh asks if Job has noticed the wings and pinions of an ostrich, and whether they are like the "kindly stork's." Job may or may not know the answer at that moment, but surely he could find out. In fact, in several places Yahweh's speeches break into straightforward descriptions—*lessons*—about creation. Surely this reveals God's great wisdom, and perhaps when it comes to the parenting habits of the ostrich, Job would not have been very well studied.

When it comes to the warhorse, it would seem that Job, as a king, would be fairly familiar with many of these details. We might also point out that some of the activities Yahweh asks Job about have been done by other human beings. Eagles and hawks can be tamed by humans (39:26–27); man has begun to search the depths of the seas (38:16); and at least one man has commanded the clouds to pour water and they have obeyed (1 Kings 17:1; cf. Josh. 5:17–18). The point of Yahweh's speeches is not to emphasize the infinite divide between Creator and creature. Though this divide most certainly and absolutely exists, Job already knows this and said so explicitly much earlier in the text (9:2–9). If this element is present, it is not front and center.

What these observations point out, however, is that while Job and the rest of humanity stand back in awe at the order, beauty, and complexity of creation and God's rule over it and care for it, God did not create the world merely to be *looked* at. Nor does he sustain all of nature only in order for man to be adequately humble. God created man to rule creation with him (Gen. 1:27–28). Even if some of the examples referred to above are debatable, at the very least we know that God created Adam to be his son, to study creation, to learn from his Father, and to rule with him. Adam was called to rule the fish of the sea, the birds of the air, the beasts of the earth, and all of creation in wisdom. He was called to learn this wisdom from his Father so that he could carry on the mission of his Father's house in the world. In other words, according to Genesis, Job may not be able to do all those things *yet*, but as a faithful son, he had better start learning.[4]

God's glory is infinite. His wisdom is infinite and it cannot be grasped. Man cannot climb up to God, but by God's grace, he can follow. This is what faithful sons do; they follow their fathers. They imitate them, follow after them, and learn their wisdom. Sons spend time with their fathers so they can learn. Whether it's changing the oil, balancing the checkbook, or doing projects around the house, sons learn from their fathers.

God has treated mankind like this from the beginning. Adam was created to learn about God's creation, to rule it wisely like God, to pick up where God left off. The psalmist says, "What is man, that you are mindful of him, the Son of Man that you remember him? You have made him a little lower than the angels and crowned him with glory and beauty" (Ps. 8:4–5). Then he gets to the point: "You have given him dominion over the works of your hands; you have put all things under his feet" (Ps. 8:6). All things have been put in subjection under man's feet, including sheep, oxen, and even the leviathan and the behemoth. God created mankind to rule with him and learn the wisdom of all these things. God is glorious, but part of his glory is his delight in his children, his sons who stand before him and learn his wisdom.

Adam was the first son, created to learn and grow up into the wisdom of God, into his whirlwind presence. Job is another Adam, another son. Job's prayer at the end of the book is proof. God says to the three friends, "You have not spoken what is right of me, but Job

---

4. These several paragraphs analyzing Keil-Delitzsch are taken substantially from my essay "Father Storm: Toward a Theology of Sons in the Book of Job" in *The Glory of Kings*.

has. And so Job can pray for you, and when he prays, I will listen." Job stands before God and is now among the sons of God in the mighty presence of God. When he prays to God, God listens. He says, "I will forgive them." He is now among those who shout for joy when God does his great deeds, and Job follows God in his glory.

James connects these themes as well. Beginning with an exhortation to patience, he summons the prophets as examples of patience and suffering. One particular example of this prophetic witness is Job: "You have heard of the steadfastness of Job, and you have seen the purpose of the Lord, how the Lord is compassionate and merciful" (Jas. 5:11). Of particular interest here is the fact that James sees Job as "steadfast" and the Lord's dealings with Job as full of compassion and mercy. On some traditional readings, Job is anything but steadfast, and Yahweh arrives just in the nick of time to pull Job back from the brink of apostasy. James, on the other hand, sees in Job an example worth following and Yahweh's dealings with him as merciful and compassionate. Yahweh does not arrive at the end to put Job in his place; Yahweh arrives to encourage Job and to bring his faith to completion.

James continues with warnings about the power of human language. Swearing frivolously may result in judgment (James 5:12). Prayer and song (in faith) participate in the magical authority of God. Those who suffer ought to pray; those who are cheerful ought to sing (James 5:13). Some who are sick ought to call for the elders to pray and anoint them. This is because "the prayer of faith will save the one who is sick, and the Lord will raise him up. And if he has committed sins, he will be forgiven" (Jas. 5:15). James runs immediately from the example of Job the prophet to prayers of faith which God promises to hear, for the forgiveness of sins, but there is more. This human standing before God and authority granted to men to call out to God and ask for mountains to be moved is exemplified in the person of Elijah. "Elijah was a man with a nature like ours, and he prayed fervently that it might not rain, and for three years and six months it did not rain on the earth. Then he prayed again, and heaven gave rain, and the earth bore its fruit" (Jas. 5:17–18). Yahweh called to Job, "Can you lift up your voice to the clouds, that a flood of waters may cover you?" (38:34) not because Job needed to remember that he was a man with a human nature and without such meteorological authority. On the contrary, Yahweh raises these questions to call Job further up and into the presence of God, to rule creation with him. Elijah had a human nature like Job, like Adam, like all of us. Yahweh's answer is the beginning of the explanation that Job has wanted.

## BEHEMOTH AND LEVIATHAN

Almost universally down through the centuries, the church has recognized in behemoth and Leviathan either an allegory or a symbol for forces or beings of evil. Gregory the Great said that Leviathan was the Satan returned from the prologue, and others have recognized the symbolic connections between Satan, "that dragon of old," and Leviathan.[5] The point Yahweh makes is something along the lines of an explanation for what has happened to Job. Yahweh plays with leviathan; Satan is Yahweh's plaything. Many other commentators dwell on these themes: all of creation, these many animals, and these final two monstrous creatures are seen as the "wild" and "dangerous" side of the universe. God, however, rules over it all perfectly. Yahweh plays with these dangerous things, and this is certainly true as far as it goes.

Many take the three friends far too seriously, giving credence to their lies, and therefore end up reading Job's complaints and accusations as primarily directed at God. This sets Yahweh's speeches up as a self-justification of his divine providence. While there are certainly hints of that in the divine speeches, we have applied many of the harshest criticisms that Job unleashes as directed at the three friends, albeit with God within earshot. Job's pleas have been for God to come and meet with him, to vindicate him, to

---

5. See Jeffrey Meyers, *Leviathan and Job, Parts 1 & 2*, Biblical Horizons Nos. 87–88. Online at http://www.biblicalhorizons.com/biblical-horizons/no-87-leviathan-and-job-part-1/
and http://www.biblicalhorizons.com/biblical-horizons/no-88-leviathan-and-job-part-2/

declare him right in front of everyone. Job is not as concerned with the presence of evil in the world per se; rather, he is concerned with the presence of evil in his courtroom (or on the ash heap) and the consequences of evil men hoisting themselves on the kingdom that Job is responsible for. From this point of view, God's control of and soverignty over the wild and dangerous things is both comforting (God is in control), but it also functions on a pedagogical level. Yahweh explains Job's educational program. In order for Job to grow up into the wisdom of his Father, he has to wrestle with wild and dangerous "beasts" just like his Father does. As Job wrestles and plays with the little dragons, the little satans, he will be prepared to wrestle with the big ones.

Not only does God play with dragons, and not only must his sons learn this life skill of taming the wild beasts of the world, but if we back up a step to see the broader context, we have to realize that there is a fundamental reason why God loves the wildness of creation. God loves the mysterious, the undomesticated, the free-spirited, because God is the original free spirit. God is not domesticated. God is not tame. The Father and the Son are bound together by the wild storm-spirit of holiness. God is a dragon, the original fire-breather. After all, the whole story of Job begins at God's instigation. It was God's idea and God's wind that struck Job's house. It was his fire that consumed the sheep and the servants, and it has ultimately been the wind-spirit of Yahweh blowing through the trials and sufferings and arguments. It was the fire of God that fell on Job's life. God is a dragon. Who can stand before him?

## Conclusion

Like Job, we are called to be sons. We've been given the Spirit of the Son, which fills us and teaches us to stand before the Father and rule the world in wisdom (Rom. 8:14–27). While there are many previews of this standing in the Old Testament, in Christ we have been raised up and seated with him in the heavenly places (Eph. 2:6). We have the Spirit-wind of the Father who teaches us to pray, to plead, and to wrestle in the hope of our redeemer who raises the dead and justifies the ungodly. This means that the original calling of Adam has been restored in Jesus. We have been restored as sons in the beloved Son, and therefore we are called to rule the beasts of the field, the fish of the seas, and the birds of the air. We are called to learn the wisdom of the Spirit that causes the wind to blow, the clouds to pour down their rain, and the stars to swing around in their courses.

Like Job, we are called to wrestle and suffer in order to learn this wisdom and to learn to rule well. This means following our crucified and risen King. We are assured that this wrestling and struggle are not only always under the rule and protection of our faithful Father, it is the exact tutorial that God has designed for us. Like the Son, we learn obedience through our suffering (Heb. 5:8), but this doesn't mean apathy. This does not mean we resign ourselves to whatever happens. Yahweh really wants us to wrestle, to wrestle with evil, to fight wickedness, and to strive with them, always looking to God for blessing. Elijah was a man with a nature like ours, and he prayed that it would not rain. The Storm has spoken his Word, and by that Word, we have been invited into the Storm to learn his wisdom.

# 11

## A Son in Glory: Job 42

We have finally come full circle and returned to the terra firma of the prose narrative. The narrator has surfaced a few times to give us brief stage directions and context, but he has finally reemerged for the conclusion of the story in all of his childish glory. The end of Job is famous; we know what happens. Job gets everything back. After all the afflictions, after all the speeches and wind, all of Job's possessions are returned. He is comforted, re-established, and lives a long life of blessing.

We know what happens, but the question is this: how does this ending fit with the rest of the story? Remember, all along, we've asked this question. We want to read the book of Job in light of the end, and now that we have finally reached the end, we want to show how this ending fits with what has come before. Many commentaries on Job cannot be bothered with asking these difficult questions and would prefer to play cut and paste with the book of Job, ascribing tensions or challenges to scribal errors, authorial oversight, or both. They are like the onlookers at Pentecost who, upon hearing something unexpected, assume that the apostles must be drunk (Acts 2:13). While this is a convenient evasion (in the case of the apostles, they were full of the Spirit), it hamstrings any attempt at understanding what the book of Job is about. What does the story mean? How does it fit in the broader biblical context? More specifically, how does the center of Job fit with the introduction and the conclusion?

In the dialogues, we have repeatedly noted how the calamities that begin in chapters 1 and 2 don't stop. The physical windstorm and firestorm stop, but the wind keeps blowing and the fire keeps burning. The three friends do not come to comfort Job; they come to accuse him. The Satan has come back in the form of three "friends." As Job is struck down in the ashes and finds himself surrounded by enemies, he cries out for death and then expands that to include a hope in a future judgment, a meeting with God. Job cries out for death, because he knows there is a judgment on the other side. He cries out for the resurrection, when his Redeemer will come to his aid and wisdom and justice will burst forth.

Whether Job anticipated a live meeting with Yahweh prior to death or not, after Elihu's speech, the Lord finally speaks to Job out of the whirlwind. The God of the storm speaks, and Job answers.

Job's response is certainly full of humility. He's humbled because he is speaking to the Lord of the universe. He is shaken and broken. Once again, it is important to note the underlying reality: "and then Job answered the Lord" (42:1; cf. 40:3). Job's friends have been telling him that this is impossible, and Job has even agreed with them (cf. 9:15, 32). On the one hand, Job has come face-to-face with God and "answered" him, which is more than perhaps he hoped for prior to death. On the other hand, Job knows he is frail and foolish, so that is what he says. Translations vary, placing particular emphasis on different connotations of the words Job uses. Again, given what God will say in several verses, affirming Job's overall approach, it seems reasonable to render Job's words accordingly.

Job affirms God's sovereignty once again, as he has before (42:2). Job is happy to admit that there are many things he does not know or understand, and he has spoken about things that are "too wonderful" for him, in direct response to Yahweh's original question about "hiding knowledge" (42:3, 38:2). Likewise, Job responds to Yahweh's statement about questioning him, and his only answer is to say that not only has he listened to God, but now he has seen God with his own eyes (42:4–5). This really is the grand culmination of what Job wanted. He wanted to meet with God and see him. This reminds us again of Jacob, who wrestled with God, saw God face-to-face, and lived (Gen. 32:30). Jacob's life was a wrestling match: wrestling with his brother in the womb, wrestling with his brother over the birthright, wrestling with his father, wrestling with his father-in-law, and finally, wrestling with the angel of the Lord face-to-face. Job has done the same thing: he begins wrestling with the calamities that befall him. Then Job wrestles with these three so-called friends, then with Elihu. Finally, he wrestles with the Lord, and he says, "My eye sees you." Like Jacob, the Lord will leave Job with tremendous blessing.

The conversation between Job and Yahweh is overwhelmingly one of blessing. Job is talking to the Lord of the universe and sees him with his eyes. He has gotten what he asked for, but what is meant when Job says, "Therefore I despise myself, and repent in dust and ashes" (42:6)? We need to be careful and not insist that Job does nothing sinful or wrong throughout the book. Job himself has admitted that if God wanted to charge him with wrong, he most certainly could (9:21), but the weight of the entire narrative is pushing us in the other direction. Job has received hardship from the Lord, withstood temptations to curse in unbelief, and instead cursing, he has resisted and wrestled with his accusers, clinging to his integrity and crying out to God for deliverance. Now, finally, he has been granted an audience with the king of the whole earth. As we noted, a great deal of Yahweh's answer is a fatherly call to his son to follow him in wisdom, to grow up into understanding, to take his stand by his Father's side in ruling creation. While we may detect elements of impatience or immaturity in Job, Yahweh's answer is not an angry rebuke. In a few verses, Yahweh affirms Job's words about him. The weight of the whole book is pushing us to say, "Job is right. Job is perfect. Job is righteous." So what is Job repenting of?

I would submit that Job is not repenting. The word here for "repent" is the word *naham* and can occasionally mean something like "repent" in the Old Testament. In the book of Job, the word is used a total of seven times, and it is otherwise never translated "repent." The other six times the word is used, it means "comfort." The three friends come to Job supposedly to "comfort" him (2:11). Later, Job accuses Eliphaz of scaring Job with his visions and dreams when Job is seeking "comfort" on his bed of mourning (or perhaps he means seeking comfort in death) (7:13). In another place Job calls the friends "miserable comforters" (16:2), and similarly he says that their words are full of falsehood and therefore their words are empty and of no "comfort" to him (21:34). Toward the end of his final speeches, he recalls, "I lived like a king among his troops, like one who comforts mourners" (29:25). In other words, the book of Job could be told as a story of a man in search of comfort. Job's friends show up, but they give him no comfort. Elihu fails to comfort Job. Finally, when Job sees God, when he speaks with God, he says that he is comforted.

The first part of 42:6 says, "Therefore I despise myself," but the word "myself" is not there in the Hebrew. The translators are trying to make sense of a verb with no object. The Hebrew literally says, "Therefore I despise"; then we have the other verb that we have just identified as probably better translated "I am comforted." There is at least one other place in the book of Job where the same verb is used with no direct object (7:16). There, translators frequently supply the words "my life" to fill in the blank. The context goes on to tell what he's talking about. Job says, "I would not live forever. Let me be alone, for my days are but a breath." He is clearly talking about his life. In 9:21, Job says the same thing explicitly: "I am blameless; I regard not myself. I loathe my life." It's the same verb; now we have the direct object explicitly provided.

In 42:6, we should do the same. Instead of adding "myself," we can add "my life," as in 7:16. Job is saying, "I'm still here in the dust and the ashes. I have still lost all ten of my children, all of my livelihood, and my kingdom is threatened on every side." Job isn't pleased with that. Nevertheless, he is comforted in the dust and ashes. In what's left of everything—the dust and ashes of the fire that has fallen from God—Job says, "I am comforted. I know everything is a mess, but my eyes have seen the Lord. I've spoken with the Lord of the universe." This reading makes sense linguistically and thematically within the context and overall thrust of the book. Job is humbled. He knows his frailty, his humanity, and that he is nothing in comparison to God, yet the Lord has brought comfort. This final response is also the final answer to the Satan. Here, Job comes face-to-face with Yahweh, and he does not curse him. Rather, he is comforted. This is the final evidence that their relationship is truly a familial father-son bond, and not merely a wooden contract.

### YAHWEH'S FINAL REPONSE (JOB 42:7–17)

The Lord says in 42:7 that his wrath is aroused against Eliphaz the Temanite and his two friends. He says, "You have not spoken of me what is right, as my servant Job has." Literally, it says that Eliphaz and Bildad and Zophar have not spoken what has been established, prepared, created by God. This is not the normal word for "right." They have not spoken what has been "established." Perhaps the idea is not only that they spoke false things, but more specifically, they have been speaking in a way that seeks to undermine God's ordering, establishing, and creating. This fits well with Yahweh's answer to Job in the whirlwind. That series of speeches specifically pointed to the created order and invited the beloved son Job into that wisdom. Job has been striving for that wisdom, looking for God his Father, crying out to speak with his Father, and Yahweh says that this is exactly right. This is pleasing; this was the point. He was inviting his son up into his glory, but the three friends have not aligned themselves with God's purpose. They have rather used the occasion to carry out their own lusts and schemes; they have tried to pull this world down. For all their theological orderliness, they have been in high rebellion against the God of heaven.

God's anger burns against the three friends for their scheming, and God orders them to offer seven bulls and seven rams (42:8). This is not a normal-sized offering; it's fairly large. In Leviticus, a sin offering for a ruler would ordinarily be a kid of the goats (Lev. 6:22–23). If the whole congregation sinned, a young bull would be offered (Lev. 6:13–14). The number seven suggests fullness and completeness, but the most prominent instance of an offering of "seven bulls and seven rams" is in the story of Balaam and Balak in Numbers 23–24. Interestingly, that episode is also concerned with blessing and cursing. Balak King of Moab has become afraid of Israel's strength coming up out of Egypt and through the wilderness, and has called upon Balaam to curse Israel so that they will no longer be a threat to him. Presumably, he hopes to defeat them in battle, but instead of cursing, Balaam blesses Israel three times and adds a fourth for good measure. Like Balak trying to get curses out of the mouth of the man of God, so too the Satan has tried unsuccessfully to get Job to curse God to his face. Yet the seven bulls and seven rams are symbolic of the nation of Israel. This is a sacrifice for an entire kingdom. In a less ambiguous context, seven bulls and seven rams are offered as sacrifices when the ark is brought into Jerusalem during David's reign (1 Chron. 15:26). Similarly, when Hezekiah cleanses the temple and restores faithful worship in Jerusalem, the rededication of the temple is marked by a large offering which includes seven bulls and seven rams (2 Chron. 29:21). These instances indicate the severity of the sin of the three friends. These three men are not normal, ordinary citizens, speaking out of ignorance; they are kings or nobles who have been plotting to steal the kingdom from Job. They have to pay; they have to offer a sacrifice suitable for an entire nation. This may also confirm Girard's suspicions that many people were led astray by the three friends in their conspiracy. This sacrifice is perhaps not only for the three friends but for the nation that has been led into sin with them. As the examples from Chronicles suggest, there is perhaps also an allusion here to the cleansing and re-dedication of Job's "house." When Yahweh speaks, not only is Job vindicated and the evil friends condemned, but the entire nation is also saved. They are delivered from the schemes of wicked men and brought back into the light of the truth.

The Lord says that Job will pray for the three friends, and the Lord will accept him (42:8). Notice that the text specifically says that Yahweh will accept *Job*. Job can pray for his three friends, so that they don't get the consequences they deserve, and the Lord will accept Job. Job is being accepted before the Lord, not them. This points to the goal toward which our story has been driving. Job, who was a great "son" in the beginning, has now graduated to the full status of "son of God." He is a prophet with access to the courts of Yahweh. When Job prays, Yahweh will hear him and accept him. Job is welcome in his presence.

Literally, the text says, "And then I will lift his face." It is Job's face that prevents Yahweh from treating the three friends as their folly merits. God will lift Job's face, and his friends will not get what they deserve. When God sees the face of Job, they will be spared. So Eliphaz the Temanite, Bildad the Shuhite, and Zophar the Naamathite did as the Lord commanded them, and the Lord accepted Job; he lifted Job's face (42:9).

These verses once again highlight Job's role as a type, a figure of the Christ who was to come and who has now come. Instead of an accuser in the presence of God, there is now an advocate with the Father. Instead of the Satan's accusations against the people of God, we now have a great High Priest who ever intercedes for us. God our Father, sees the face of Jesus, the beloved son, and when the Father sees his face, he hears our prayers and answers from heaven. The Satan indeed has been cast down from heaven, and now Jesus is seated at the right hand of the Father. Not only that: we, like Job, are called to a ministry of reconciliation, a ministry that includes and even highlights praying for our enemies and blessing those who persecute us. Jesus, as the greater Job, suffered and died and rose again in order to turn his enemies into friends. Jesus died and rose again out of love for the world, so that we who were once enemies might be brought near and forgiven. Job prefigures this glorious gospel in his prayers of intercession for the three friends. Job prays for his enemies, and God relents from the destruction they deserve. The tables have been dramatically turned. Job is now being reinstated as a king, and the three friends are at his mercy. Instead of sentencing them to death, which all traitors ordinarily deserve, Job prays for their forgiveness. While we are not told, one wonders what sort of effect this treatment of enemies may have had on them. What did these "burning coals" heaped on their heads do?

Regardless of exactly what happened after the close of the story, notice how the word "friends" has come full circle. When they first arrived in the guise of "comforters" it was easy to believe that they meant what they said. It was hard to believe that they meant Job any ill will. As the dialogues went on, however, and as we read Job carefully, we realized just how dark their intentions were. The "friends" were really enemies, and they were full of malicious accusations. They were little satans, full of the lies of their father the Devil. Now, at long last, the truth has been declared. Yahweh has proclaimed their guilt and Job's innocence and righteousness. Here, where it has all come to light, Yahweh invites Job to pray for these enemies as though they were his friends. The friends (who were really enemies) have now been *declared* enemies so that Job can pray for them like friends.

Job is a beloved son of the Lord. God loves Job, and when Job prays to him, God answers. Yahweh literally "returns the captivity of Job" (42:10). Most translations say that God restored Job's losses or fortunes, but the word means "captivity" or "exile." God returns the captivity of Job. Job has been in exile, enslaved by the calamities, enslaved by the three friends, estranged from his family and friends. When Job prays for the friends, God returns the captivity of Job (42:10), and this means that Yahweh gives Job double what he had previously. Whenever God brings his son out of slavery, he brings him out with riches (Gen. 13:1–2; 20:14; Ex. 12:35–36; Ezra 1:6). So even here, Job's family and friends gather around him to eat and bring him presents of money and rings of gold (42:11).

We see something similar in Zechariah 9:11–12 when God returns the captivity of Israel and restores to them double. Here, 11,000 sheep, camels, and donkeys means 22,000 of the same restored. Job gets exactly double of all of those possessions: cattle, sheep, oxen, camels (42:12). This restoration from exile is also a resurrection scene. Or, perhaps what we ought to say, is that resurrection is always a doubling. When a man comes back from the dead, he receives another life, life doubled. Here, Job receives his ten children back: seven sons and three daughters, the exact numbers, as though they have returned from the grave (42:13).

The doubling of Job's possessions might suggest a couple of other things to us. First, returning double is a form of restitution. In the law, double return is required for anything that's stolen or lost (Ex. 22:4–9). It can include very intentional burglary, but it can also include any lost thing that comes up before the judges. Of course, there is no guilt on Yahweh's part. He is restoring Job's livelihood in a manner that is far above reproach. He was not personally guilty of theft, but the Lord restores double, like a friend who cares. He restores twice what is lost. Another connection is the fact that the double portion is an inheritance (Deut. 21:17). Remember the firstborn son? That's what Jacob and Esau fought over. The firstborn son receives a double portion of the inheritance. Why does the firstborn son receive a double portion of the father's inheritance? Is he just lucky? The firstborn son receives a double portion of his father's inheritance because it's the son's job both to care for his parents when his parents grow old, and to carry on his father's household. The double portion is the means that will enable him to carry on the mission of his father's house. His father has a kingdom, an estate that needs to be run, and so the firstborn son was the one chosen to run the estate, and he would need resources. The Lord restores to Job a firstborn inheritance. Job is a beloved firstborn son of God, and these double portions are the resources that he will need to carry on his Father's mission in the world.

Resurrection is always glorification. It's life back from the dead, twice the life back from the dead, and better, more glorious, and more beautiful. This is illustrated in Job's daughters. Here in the conclusion of the story, the narrator goes into much greater detail than we had in the beginning. Job's sons remain nameless, but his daughters are named and we are told that they are the most beautiful daughters in all of the land (42:14–15). Not only this, but Job gives his three daughters an inheritance among their brothers. In other words, Job gives them an inheritance of sons. In Job's family, there is neither male nor female.

Like Job, Jesus has also returned from exile. Jesus has returned from the exile of the grave. When Jesus was raised from the dead, "he led captivity captive and gave gifts to men." When Jesus was returned from exile, he broke the curse of exile wide open. He made the way of escape, and collected his inheritance from his Father (Ps. 2). Having collected the inheritance, he poured out the Spirit-wind full of gifts upon his people. Jesus is the true Son of God, the true Firstborn, and the firstborn from the dead. Jesus has received the double portion of the Spirit so that he might be faithful in all of his Father's house. He has poured out that same Spirit on us so that we all with him might be firstborn sons, carrying on the mission of our Father's house in the world.

Of course, Job's restoration-resurrection scene is only a faint glimmer of what we are witnesses to in Jesus. It's just a glimmer put in perspective by the last verse of the book. Job died, old and full of days (42:16–17). Job wrestled with God, obsessed with the blessing of God, and God poured out enormous blessings on Job, but he still died.

We are like Job, all of us. This side of the final resurrection, we still look forward to glory. We look forward to final restoration. We look forward to the inheritance of the sons of God (Rom. 8:19ff). All Christians have been given the Spirit of the Son, and that is why we cry out to God as our Father (Matt. 6:9; Rom. 6:15). "For all who are led by the Spirit of God are sons of God" (Rom. 8:14). That Spirit within us groans and looks forward to the redemption of the sons of God, and all of creation groans with us, looking forward to the final restoration and resurrection. This means walking in hope. It means setting our eyes on Jesus, the faithful Son, who has gone before us, who has already been raised to the right hand of God the Father, who has already been given an inheritance. You are his inheritance. Jesus is the greater Elisha who received a double portion of the Spirit and poured out that gift on the Church at Pentecost. He calls us to follow him as faithful sons, walking in hope, in perseverance, like Job.

This hope, as we've seen, is not numb to pain. Job was not unfaithful or unrighteous to cry out in his agony. Faithful sons cry out to God. They feel pain and hardship. They hope in their Father. Faithful sons hope and rest in the comfort of the storm. The Lord is a storm. He has poured out his storm presence on you in his Spirit, and that storm is at work in our lives, refashioning us, remaking us, and remaking the entire world, until the earth has been covered with his glory and with his knowledge, as the waters cover the sea.

That process is not always fun. Job did not have a lot of fun, but his ending is glorious. It's very good. It's wonderful, and beauty beyond compare; the end of the story is resurrection. The question is not whether everything is "fun." The question Christians must ask themselves is, "Am I walking in the comfort of the storm?" When you speak to your children, do they sense that you are comforted by the God of the storm? Or do they sense that you are caught up and running around crazy in the storm? When you speak to your neighbors, when you speak to your wife, do they know that you are grounded in the comfort of the storm?

Though there is dust and ashes all around, though the storm has wreaked its havoc, all who trust in the Son of God have the Spirit of God speak the Father, the Lord of the storm, and he promises to listen and answer. You are a son of the Father. You are a beloved son of the God of the storm, and his Spirit is drawing you in love into his glory.

www.ingramcontent.com/pod-product-compliance
Lightning Source LLC
Chambersburg PA
CBHW071919290426
44110CB00013B/1409